CINEMAS OF HARINGEY

by Jeremy Buck

Hornsey Historical Society

Published by
Hornsey Historical Society
The Old Schoolhouse
136 Tottenham Lane
London N8 7EL

www.hornseyhistorical.org.uk

Registered Charity No. 274424

ISBN No. 978-0-905794-41-9

© Hornsey Historical Society and Jeremy Buck, 2010

First printing: October 2010

Book design: Mike Hazeldine

Front cover: The Muswell Hill Electric Theatre, later Summerland Cinema, photographed soon after opening in 1912. *(Cinema Theatre Association Archive) See pages 52 to 55*

Title pages: A fashion contest on the stage of the Gaumont Wood Green in the 1950s, showing the Compton organ. *(Authors collection) See inside front cover*

Contents page: The Electric Palace on Highgate Hill photographed in 1922. *(Islington Local History Centre) See page 50*

Back cover: A present day picture of the Muswell Hill Odeon showing the striking neon display at night. *(Conrad Williams) See pages 58 to 65*

Contents

Introduction

One of my strongest childhood memories is of going each week to the special children's Saturday morning picture shows at the Odeon Cinema, Wood Green in the 1960s. Although I could sense the cinema was an imposing, grand structure with a large number of seats, I didn't realise that it was of such architectural interest that it was later to gain a Grade II* listing. The Borough of Haringey is fortunate in having two other listed cinema buildings within its borders, namely the Odeon at Muswell Hill, also listed Grade II*, and the Palace at Tottenham, listed Grade II, which although it started as a live variety theatre, has spent much of its life showing films. As well as these nationally appreciated buildings, there were scores of other cinema buildings in the borough which, whilst not so glamorous or well-known, provided their patrons with many hours of cheap entertainment in the heyday of cinema-going in the 1930s and 1940s. I hope this book will bring back memories of some of these well-loved cinemas and also give some indication to those who were not there, of how important "going to the pictures" once was for so many people.

I must thank all those who have willingly contributed their memories, which appear throughout the book. The main sources of factual information are listed in the references section at the rear.

Jeremy Buck, 2010

From Cinematographe to Multiplex

It may be useful to have a brief general outline of the development of cinema building in England, so that local buildings can be set in context.

The first public demonstration of cinema in the UK, as we would recognise it, took place on February 20th 1896 when, at the Regent Street Polytechnic, London, Felicien Trewey presented the Lumiere Brothers films which had premiered the previous year in Paris. This was really more of a scientific demonstration than a cinema show, mainly to members of the press and other guests. The audience was allegedly greatly surprised, even alarmed, by scenes such as a train arriving at a station, because they had never seen moving pictures on such a scale before. Their early experiences would have been limited to the fairground attractions we came to know as "What the Butler Saw" machines. The Lumiere films went under the title "Cinematographe" and the word "cinema" was born, alternatively spelt as "kinema". "Bioscope" or "Biograph" were amongst the other early terms used to describe the new experience.

Within a short period, the films received a much wider audience when they became part of the bill at the Empire Theatre, a music hall in Leicester Square, and later other films by other pioneers also came to be shown at the adjacent Alhambra music hall. From these humble beginnings, Leicester Square has remained the hub of the cinema business in London's West End. What was seen as a passing fad in the music-hall proprietors soon became more popular than the live acts, and, in time, cinema would be a contributory factor in the decline of the music halls where it had first appeared.

The popularity of moving pictures continued to grow, and

shows started in a variety of hastily converted premises such as shops and public halls, etc. as well as becoming an attraction at travelling fairs. Many of these early films were of a factual nature, and quite short, with longer, fictional films coming later. The early projectors' shortcomings meant that the films often "flickered" when shown on the screen, hence "flicks" which became a popular term for the cinema. The earliest shows in our area were in public halls in Wood Green and Tottenham.

The problem with these early building conversions was that film stock was flammable, and could get jammed in the primitive projectors and catch fire from the heat of the lamp, generally a naked carbon arc flame. The resulting smoke and flames would instil panic into the usually overcrowded auditorium and there would be a rush for the often inadequate exits. There were several cases of people being killed in the crush following such an outbreak, and this led to a call to introduce some regulation to the burgeoning cinema business.

Finsbury Park Cinematograph Theatre, pictured in 1914.
(Reproduced by permission of English Heritage. NMR)

6

The resulting Cinematograph Act of 1909 came into force on January 1st 1910, and this resulted in a large number of purpose-built cinema buildings being constructed. It is estimated that by 1913, there were 497 buildings being used as cinemas in London alone. Most of the earlier converted premises had to close, because the Act's main requirements were that the projector equipment had to be housed in a separate room from the audience, behind a solid wall with glazed apertures for the projector's beams to shine through, which could be closed by metal shutters if a fire should occur. There also had to be improved emergency exits and fire-fighting equipment. In the local area, the Act was enforced by the Middlesex County Council until 1965, and they issued licences annually, and regularly inspected each cinema. Several of our local cinemas opened in 1910 and 1911 as a result of the Act.

After an inevitable interruption during the First World War, cinema attendances continued to grow, and larger cinemas started to be built. The early buildings had generally seated between 400 to 600, but by the 1920s cinemas seating around 1000 or more began to appear. The Cinema in Bruce Grove, Tottenham opened in 1921 and had nearly 1800 seats.

Early cinemas had often been built and operated by individuals, but right from the start, there were small chains of cinemas. The Cinematograph Theatre opened in 1909 at Finsbury Park was part of a chain, as was the Premier Electric at Harringay of 1910. Later, in the 1930s, large national chains started to emerge, the most familiar names being Odeon, Gaumont and ABC, all represented locally. Other smaller chains were Essoldo and Granada. These chains generally built new cinemas from scratch- such as the Odeon at Muswell Hill and the Gaumont at Wood Green, but sometimes they took over existing buildings – such as The Rink at Finsbury Park and the Palace, Tottenham, both operated by Gaumont.

With the development of sound films from 1929 onwards, cinemas had to modify their projection equipment, and fit speakers behind the screen. This involved some considerable expense, and although most of the local cinemas adapted for sound, a few closed in the 1920s, unable to finance the conversion and unable to compete with those cinemas who could.

The staff of the Odeon, Muswell Hill pose for the photographer soon after opening in
1936. The manager and his assistant are in evening dress in the centre, commissionaires
/doormen in their uniform and hats, ladies in uniform are usherettes, ladies without
uniform are the cashiers, the men in white coats are the projection staff, and the lady in
the white hat worked in the café. *(Reproduced by permission of English Heritage.NMR)*

The new buildings of the 1930s were characterised by
their luxurious fittings and decorative treatment, often in the
popular "art deco" style. Some were on a large scale, with over
2500 seats. They often had added features such as cafes and
restaurants, occasionally dance-halls attached, and were
equipped with the latest in theatre entertainment – a "Wurlitzer"
pipe organ, imported from the USA, or a British-built equivalent,
such as a "Compton".

Prior to 1929, when films had been silent, they were
generally accompanied by a pianist or by someone playing a
"straight" church-like organ. In the larger cinemas, a small
orchestra provided the music. But as the expense of providing
these orchestras rose, the theatre organ – a more versatile form
of pipe organ – was developed in America, to provide an
alternative. By the time these organs arrived here in the mid-
1920s and early 1930s, sound films were being developed, but

The Wurlitzer pipe organ formerly installed in the Palace, Tottenham, in its present location at Rye College, Rye.

(Glen Twamley)

The Compton pipe organ formerly installed in the Gaumont, Wood Green, in its present location at Thorngate Hall, Gosport.

(Peter Staveley)

organs continued to be installed up until the late 1930s to entertain patrons during the interval. The Palace, Tottenham, had a very early Wurlitzer installed, whilst the Gaumont at Wood Green had a Compton.

During the Second World War, and into the 1940s and early 1950s, cinema attendances remained very high and these were probably the "boom" years for the industry, when the highest number of admissions was recorded. For a large number of people a visit to the pictures was a weekly ritual, and for many people, more frequently than that. It provided a relatively cheap form of entertainment, unlike the live theatre which was more expensive, and perceived as more suitable for the "upper-classes" – whereas anyone could visit the cinema, and you didn't need to dress up to go.

By the late 1950s, a decline had started- brought about largely by the development of television which meant people could stay at home and be entertained. Cinemas started to close in large numbers – many were converted for the latest craze of bingo, but a lot of them were demolished or otherwise redeveloped. Attempts were made to stem the decline by introducing new features such as larger screens, Cinemascope and 70mm films, and films in 3D. But by the 1960s, the large auditoriums which had once been so busy were proving difficult to fill, and could appear cold and unwelcoming to the reduced number of patrons. So cinemas started to be subdivided into smaller, more intimate spaces, thus also offering a wider choice of films at each site. This happened to local cinemas at Muswell Hill, Wood Green and Turnpike Lane.

This development did not really stem the decline, but a new development, copied from the USA, started in Milton Keynes in 1985- the multiplex cinema. This consisted of a new building, containing a large number of small cinemas thus providing a greater choice of film. "The Point" at Milton Keynes had 10 screens, but later examples often had more than this. These multiplexes are often associated with adjacent restaurants and other entertainments, and generally require a large piece of land, as they rely on people coming in their cars, so initially none were constructed in Haringey. There were several around the edge of the borough, for example at Edmonton and Finchley. But in 2000, a 12-screen multiplex was constructed in the heart of Wood Green, which had been without a cinema since 1984. Here, customers could utilise the existing car parks constructed for shoppers. This was followed soon after by another multiplex a few yards away which, although without parking, is well placed for public transport access.

Despite great advances in home entertainment – DVDs, wide-screen digital televisions and surround-sound systems- cinema attendances remain buoyant but nowhere like their heyday in the 1940s. From this author's experience, cinemas are often poorly attended during the week, only becoming busy between Friday evening and Sunday.

Today the only "traditional "cinema still open for business in Haringey is the Odeon at Muswell Hill which has been serving the local population since 1936.

HOW THIS BOOK IS ARRANGED

Cinemas have been grouped into six sections each covering a different area of the Borough. In each section, the main cinemas are described in the approximate order that they opened. The original name is given first, followed by subsequent re-namings. Modern-day postcodes are given to enable identification of the site.

Opening and closing dates are summarised at the start, then details of the subsequent use of the site, followed by a general description of the architecture and history of the cinema. In most cases this is followed by recollections from people who either worked at the cinema or went to see films there.

Then there follows a description of other local buildings which also showed films.

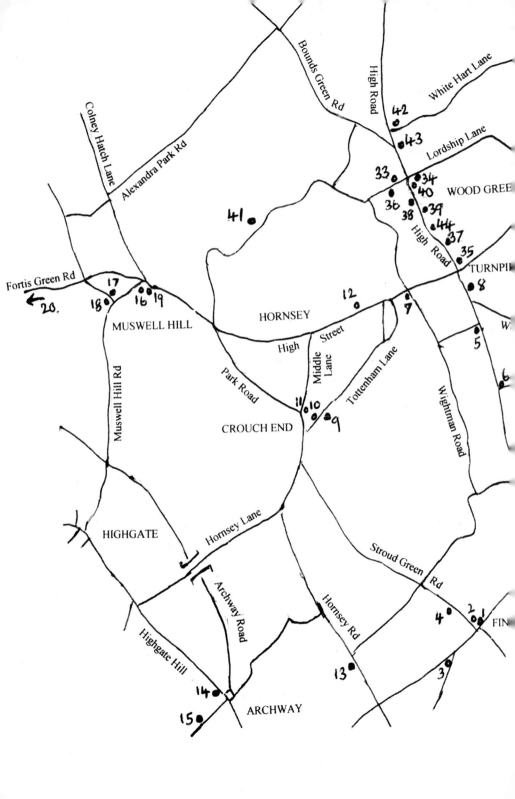

CINEMAS OF HARINGEY

Finsbury Park
1. CINEMATOGRAPH
2. RINK/GAUMONT
3. ASTORIA/ODEON
4. SCALA

Harringay
5. PREMIER/REGAL/ESSOLDO/CURZON
6. ELECTRIC COLISEUM/COLISEUM
7. GRAND/NEW CLARENCE/REGENT
8. RITZ/ABC/CANNON/CORONET

Hornsey , Crouch End & Highgate
9. PICTURE HOUSE/PERFECT/PLAZA
10. HIPPODROME
11. ASSEMBLY ROOMS (Crouch End)
12. NATIONAL HALL
13. HORNSEY PALACE/STAR
14. ELECTRIC PALACE/PALACE
15. ODEON (Highgate)

Muswell Hill
16. MUSWELL HILL ELECTRIC/SUMMERLAND
17. ATHENAEUM
18. ODEON (Muswell Hill)
19. RITZ/ABC
20. PHOENIX

Tottenham
21. PEOPLES PALACE
22. CANADIAN RINK
23. CENTRAL HALL/ ROXY/MAYFAIR
24. HOTSPUR
25. WYVERN/TOTTENHAM CINEMA
26. CORNER
27. GRAND/PAVILION/FLORIDA
28. IMPERIAL/ESSOLDO
29. BRUCE GROVE
30. TOTTENHAM PALACE
31. STUDIOS 5,6,7,8
32. MUNICIPAL BATHS HALL

Wood Green
33. ELECTROSCOPE/PALAIS DELUXE/REX
34. LORDSHIP LANE CINEMATOGRAPH
35. WOOD GREEN ELECTRIC/CROWN
36. CENTRAL/NEW CENTRAL
37. PICTURE PALLADIUM/PALLADIUM
38. GAUMONT PALACE/ODEON
39. CINEWORLD
40. SHOWCASE/VUE
41. ALEXANDRA PALACE THEATRE
42. ASSEMBLY ROOOMS (Wood Green)
43. STUART HALL
44. WOOD GREEN EMPIRE

Finsbury Park

FINSBURY PARK CINEMATOGRAPH THEATRE

269 Seven Sisters Road, Finsbury Park, N4 2DE

Opened 2nd October 1909. Closed 1918.
Became entrance hall of adjoining Rink Cinema
(see that section for subsequent history)
Demolished 1999, LIDL Supermarket on site.

This early cinema was the second in a small chain of London cinemas – eventually numbering 16 – developed by Montagu Pyke. In his autobiography, written in the 1930s, he recalls: "Next came the Finsbury Park cinema. I leased the ground site of the old tramway sheds at Finsbury Park Gates, pulled these down, and erected a picture theatre to seat 500. Of course the ground space I had rented was much greater than I needed, so I let the tremendous back part to somebody else who built a roller skating rink. The great luxury cinema called the Finsbury Park Empire, holding some 3000 seats, stands on the site of the skating rink today and the space where my cinema originally stood now serves as a handsome entrance lobby." (Pyke is mistaken in saying that the large cinema adjacent to his was called the Empire – that was the name of a music hall in nearby St Thomas' Road).

Pyke generally formed a separate limited company for each of his cinemas – here it was the Finsbury Park Cinematograph Theatre Company. Later several of these companies were merged to form Amalgamated Cinematograph Theatres Limited (ACT).

The front of the Cinematograph Theatre (see page 6) was richly decorated, with elaborate plasterwork and large lamps. As this was one of the first cinemas to be built anywhere, the architects – Horace Gilbert and Stephanos Constanduras – had nothing much to copy. They were therefore probably influenced by the travelling fairground filmshows where many early cinema presentations had taken place – these had often had a large, brightly coloured frontage to draw patrons in. Generally the hall behind this front was very basic, often just a large tent. At Pyke's hall, the auditorium was quite narrow and basic on a single, sloping floor, with around 650 seats. It was decorated, according to the description in "The Bioscope" magazine, "in green, pink and terracotta, and well ventilated by 14 air shafts and 8 small electrical fans". The fibrous plasterwork and decorations, both inside and on the frontage, were by Boekbinder of Kentish Town. At the opening show, there was incidental music "rendered by Mr W Draper on organ and piano" – the organ was probably a portable harmonium-type instrument. The actual film programme is not described.

Being in a good position by a railway station, a tram route and the park gates, business was good. But unfortunately for Pyke, the roller skating rink that had been built next door was fairly soon turned into a cinema, with greater seating capacity and superior facilities. This naturally drew business away from the smaller Pyke's hall and, combined with the effects of the War- meaning shortages of staff and of film product – led to the collapse of Pyke's business empire in 1915, and the cinema closed. The ACT Company was however reconstituted in 1915, and reopened the Finsbury Park cinema and managed it until it closed in 1918.

This was not the end of the building's use for entertainment however, because the owners of the adjacent Rink cinema wanted a more prominent frontage in a busier road, so converted Pyke's building into an impressive entrance hall for their cinema.

The frontage was remodelled, and a balcony was inserted inside forming a large café/restaurant. The new entrance opened in May 1920 – further information is given in the Rink Cinema section.

Pyke's cinema was to remain an entrance hall for the next 64 years – first for cinema, then dancing, then bingo, when "one-armed bandit" gaming machines lined its walls. In 1984, when bingo ceased, it was boarded up, with occasional use as a retail unit, before sudden demolition in 1999. The site remained vacant until a LIDL supermarket was built around 2006.

The Cinematograph Theatre frontage rebuilt as the entrance to Finsbury Park Cinema, pictured in 1923. "Dempsey v Firpo" is a film of a boxing match.

(Reproduced by permission of English Heritage. NMR)

The auditorium of the Cinematograph Theatre after conversion to the entrance hall of the Finsbury Park Cinema, pictured in 1923.

(Reproduced by permission of English Heritage. NMR)

FINSBURY PARK RINK CINEMA / FINSBURY PARK CINEMA / RINK / GAUMONT

10 Stroud Green Road, Finsbury Park, N4 2DF
(with entrance later at 269 Seven Sisters Road)

Opened (for films) 14th July 1913. Closed 12th July 1958.
Became a ballroom, then a bingo club,
now a ten-pin bowling and pool club.

This building, in the far south-west corner of the Borough, has successfully adapted itself to meet the changing fashions in popular entertainment. Over the years it has housed roller-skating, billiards, films, dancing, boxing, pop concerts, bingo, snooker, bowling and pool.

It first opened on 26th January 1910 as the Finsbury Park Rink, constructed on the site of a horse-tram depot, and owned by Premier Rinks Ltd. The architects were Fair, Mayer and Marshall. A billiard room was also included in the building, and there were promenades around the roller-skating rink for spectators and a spacious balcony with a decorative front.

Roller-skating – or "rinking" – had been a craze since around 1908, and several large rinks were built across London to cater for demand. One had opened nearby at Wood Green just a few days before Finsbury Park, and one at Tottenham opened the following month. This was not just plain skating, but featured themed evenings such as Carnival Nights, Novelty Nights, Fancy-Dress Contests, etc – more of a social occasion than a leisure or sporting event.

"De-Luxe" was added to Finsbury Park's name soon after opening, but unfortunately the skating craze proved to be short-lived. The Rink had closed by 1911, and after a short period as a dance hall- "Palais De Dance" – was acquired by Messrs Goodwin and Evans, directors of North Metropolitan Theatres Ltd, to rebuild for films. This was the latest craze, which proved to be longer lasting!

The architect Edward A Stone, of the company of Norfolk

& Prior, was engaged for the rebuilding. Stone (1880-1963) was a shareholder and trustee of North Metropolitan Theatres. He was involved in the design or re-building of other local cinemas, such as the Central at Stamford Hill, the Canadian Rink at Tottenham and the Crouch End Hippodrome. Later, he would become a very prolific cinema and theatre designer, responsible for the Finsbury Park Astoria (just over the Islington border) and the Prince Edward and Whitehall theatres in London's West End amongst many others.

Interior of the Finsbury Park Cinema, pictured in 1923. Notice the pipe organ on left-hand balcony. *(Reproduced by permission of English Heritage. NMR)*

At Finsbury Park, Stone remodelled the entrance into a "winter garden" complete with fountain, statuary, foliage and lounge chairs, and the bare steel trusses of the rink roof were covered by a more elegant barrel-vaulted plaster ceiling. The promenades became waiting areas, the balcony was rearranged to include a projection room constructed to house the film projectors, and 2,800 seats were provided for the patrons.

On opening in July 1913, a typical programme would consist of an hour and a half of films and an hour of variety given by the Rink Costume Concert Party.

The new cinema seemed to have prospered, even during the First World War, and around 1915, a Thomas Jones pipe organ was installed to accompany the films. On June 4th 1919, a fire broke out in the auditorium which caused the cinema to be closed until 1920, although the winter garden and café continued to operate. By then the proprietors were Associated Provincial Picture Houses (APPH), and during the closure they undertook improvements to the building, including an expansion into the vacant Cinematograph Theatre, closed since 1918, with its entrance on Seven Sisters Road. This space was restyled as a foyer and café, meaning the Rink could have a more prominent street presence. In the auditorium, seating capacity was reduced slightly to 2,012.

The cinema was renamed Finsbury Park Cinema and reopened on 17th May 1920. In 1923, it became the first cinema in Britain to give a demonstration, to the trade, of talking films- the "Phonofilms" system of sound-on-film, later developed as Fox "Movietone". It would be a further 5 years before the first talking picture was shown to the public.

In July 1926, the Jones organ was removed and the latest novelty – a Wurlitzer theatre organ- was installed instead. This was a 2 manual, 8-rank Model F – only the ninth such organ to be imported from the USA – leaving the Wurlitzer factory in North Tonawanda in May 1926. The organists at the opening were billed as John T. Thompson and a "Mr Young".

In February 1929, APPH and its parent company, Provincial Cinematograph Theatres, were acquired by the Gaumont-British Corporation. This was one of the first acquisitions of the growing Gaumont circuit, which would eventually become one of the leading chains alongside Odeon and ABC. The word "Rink" was inserted into the cinema's name again by 1936, with "a Gaumont-British Theatre" added in advertising.

During World War II, the cinema suffered slight damage, and the Wurlitzer organ was removed. It was put into store, but later broken down for spare parts for other organs.

On 14th August 1950, the name "Rink" was dropped in

(Above)
The Finsbury Park/Rink
Cinema pictured in 1950 just
before it was renamed
Gaumont.

(Cinema Museum, London)

(Left)
The Finsbury Park/ Rink
Cinema pictured in 1945.

*(Cinema Theatre Association
Archive)*

20

favour of plain "Gaumont" to give the circuit a more unified profile. But the cinema closed in July 1958 with two unremarkable films: *Undersea Girl* starring Mara Corday and *Fraulein* featuring Mel Ferrer. This was due to a general decline in audiences, and also because the newly-rebuilt Gaumont at nearby Holloway was to re-open, after suffering war damage, on 21st July 1958, and the Rank Organisation – who by now controlled the Gaumont circuit – wished to build an audience at that cinema after 14 years of closure. Rank also operated the

The Finsbury Park Cinema/Rink entrance rebuilt as the entrance to Top Rank Bingo, pictured in the 1970s *(Cinema Theatre Association archive)*

nearby Finsbury Park Astoria, and probably felt there were too many local cinemas for them all to operate at a profit.

The building was converted to a dance-hall, the New Majestic Ballroom, later referred to as plain Majestic, which opened on 20th August 1959. Boxing and wrestling matches were also held on several occasions between 1960 and 1964, and pop acts also performed – notably The Beatles on April 24th 1963.

In 1961 bingo started to be the attraction on 2 or 3 evenings per week, alongside "jive nights" for teenagers and wrestling on other nights, and by 1964 the ballroom closed and was converted to a full-time Top Rank bingo hall. The balcony area was partitioned off by a wall and became a snooker club using the Stroud Green Road entrance. Patrons for bingo used the Seven Sisters Road entrance. Bingo lasted until September 1984 – a new Top Rank club opened in the former Gaumont at Wood Green, and to build up attendances there, Finsbury Park, as well as the bingo at the former Regal Edmonton, were closed.

The Seven Sisters Road entrance was boarded up and left empty until demolition in 1999. Snooker continued at the Stroud Green Road end, and later the former cinema auditorium became a health and fitness club, and is now Rowans ten-pin bowling and pool centre (pool being a billiard-like game, not swimming).

David Goodman (writing in *Picture House* magazine in 2000) worked as a sound manager at the Rink in 1930:
"We were called sound managers because in the early days of the talkies, they didn't know much about it and they wanted technical people. It was a lot of business going on with the projection of sound- it had to be checked every morning to make sure the light was concentrated on the soundtrack. I was at the Rink for about 6 months during which time at the Empire round the corner, the Tiller Girls were appearing – there were several different troupes of these girls. One of the girls used to come over to the café at the Rink and I got on with her and we used to go out together. What could she have seen in me? I think she was looking for a meal ticket, out for a good time. Then all of a sudden the Company said they were going to send me out on relief – I went touring all over the country- ending up at Bradford for 6 months. By that time the Tiller girl had

gone to Rome- she used to write but I gradually dropped it!" (David Goodman later became the manager at the Gaumont, Wood Green – see later section)

Hilda Hewitt, (writing in 2008 when she lived in Tottenham) recalls:
"I used to go to the Rink in Finsbury Park and of course it was a skating rink before a cinema. They had a "Talent Night" on Friday or Saturday evening when the public were invited to perform on stage – e.g. sing or play a musical instrument as well as watch two films and the news. There were a lot of cinemas in Tottenham as well – the Palace in the High Road, and the Florida. On Saturday mornings there was children's cinema at the Palace and at the ABC Turnpike Lane. My younger son seldom went as it was too noisy and children ran around the cinema!"

Other places in the area where films were shown:

ASTORIA / ODEON

232-8, Seven Sisters Road, Finsbury Park, N4 3NX

Located just over the Islington border, this large cinema, with over 3,000 seats, was designed by Edward A. Stone, and opened on 29th September 1930. The plain tiled exterior, whilst impressive, hides a more magnificent interior, designed by Somerford & Barr, in the "atmospheric" style. This is meant to give the audience the impression that they are sitting outside, under a warm Spanish sky. The ceiling is plain blue, pierced by electric twinkling stars, and to each side of the stage are miniature houses, courtyards, fountains and trailing plants to create the illusion. The foyers are lavishly decorated, complete with a fountain containing goldfish.

The Astoria was operated by Paramount from 1931, then acquired by the Odeon chain in 1939, but not renamed Odeon until 1970. It closed for films in 1971, and became the Rainbow Theatre for live acts, particularly rock and pop music, fondly remembered by many people. This lasted until 1981, and after a long period of disuse and decay, the cinema has been restored to its former glory by current occupiers, the religious group UCKG. It is listed at Grade II*. In February 2004, the Cinema Theatre Association presented the film *Sunset Boulevard* and returned the Astoria to a cinema for one night only.

SCALA

15 The Parade, Stroud Green Road, Finsbury Park, N4 2AL

The border between Haringey and Islington runs down the centre of Stroud Green Road, and on the Islington side was the Scala opened in October 1914. The architect was H.W. Horsley who provided a 706-seat auditorium for owners Jackson & Hanks. It became the New Scala in 1920, but shortly afterwards the nearby Rink Cinema was rebuilt with enlarged capacity and superior facilities, and the smaller cinema could not compete for long. It closed in 1924, and was converted to a factory. This closed and was demolished in 2007, and housing now occupies the site.

Harringay

PREMIER ELECTRIC / PREMIER / REGAL / ESSOLDO / CURZON / NEW CURZON

92 Frobisher Road Harringay N8 0QX

Opened 16th April 1910. Closed 10th November 1963.
Became a bingo club.
Re-opened 15th February 1964. Closed 1989.
Became a laser game centre.
Re-opened 31st October 1997. Closed January 2003.
Became a place of worship.

This is the oldest purpose-built cinema building in the Borough which still exists, and one of the oldest in London. It was still showing films as recently as 2003, a period spanning almost 93 years, although with some breaks.

It opened in 1910 as part of a small circuit operated by Premier Electric Theatres Ltd, which also had cinemas at Woolwich, Earlsfield and Leytonstone. The architects were the firm of Emden and Egan. They provided an interesting façade, with touches of the Orient about it, and a simple auditorium with a barrel-vaulted ceiling decorated by plaster foliage. There were seats for 900 patrons – a fairly tight squeeze. Early advertising says that "the Premier Orchestra will perform popular descriptive music at all performances" and "Afternoon Tea will be served Free of Charge at matinees". All this for a top price of only one shilling (5p). Amongst the early films projected on to the small screen (painted on to the back wall) were *The Kidnapped Servant* and *The Road Agent*. These films are listed without star names – the concept of "film stars" did not arise until later on.

The Premier Electric, Harringay, pictured in 1927.
(Bruce Castle Museum (Haringey Culture, Libraries and Learning))

A postcard of Queens Head, Harringay, showing Premier Electric Cinema on the right.
(Hugh Flouch collection)

The interior of the Premier Electric, photographed in 1938 as work began to modernise the building into the Regal

(Cinema Theatre Association Archive)

The cinema continued to thrive, and was adapted for sound films in September 1930, when the name was shortened to just "Premier" to give a more modern feel. In January 1938, the owner became Harry Pearl, who traded as Gaywood Cinemas, who also owned the nearby Palais De Luxe in Wood Green. The cinema had faced stiff competition since 1935 from the Ritz which had opened very close by, adjacent to the new Turnpike Lane tube station. Gaywood decided they had to modernize to compete, and they closed the Premier in January 1938 for a complete modernisation. Renowned cinema architect Frederic E Bromige was engaged to provide a new frontage to the cinema in the popular art-deco style – well forward of the old front – and the foyer was modernised to look more streamlined. A new screen was erected in front of the old painted one and the ribs of the barrel-vault ceiling were smoothed over, as were the foliage-clad walls. This modernisation was achieved in just under 6 weeks!

A more modern name was needed and so on 7th March 1938 it re-opened as the Regal, with the film *The Sky's the Limit* starring Jack Buchanan. Seating capacity had been reduced to a more comfortable 649.

The modernisation seemed to have paid off, as the cinema continued for a further 25 years before the general decline brought about its closure. It was acquired by Southan Morris cinemas in 1948, and then in 1954 by the Essoldo circuit, and it was renamed Essoldo in 1959. It was sub-let to Broadmead

(Above)
The Premier / Regal / Curzon pictured in 1970 showing the art-deco frontage erected 30 years earlier in front of the original 1910 façade.

(Kevin Wheelan)

(Left)
Interior of the Premier/Regal photographed in 1984.

(Martin Dusashenka)

Entertainments in October 1963, but it closed two months later, on 10th December 1963 with the film *Circus of Horrors* starring Anton Diffring.

It was converted to a bingo club, named Vogue, but there were only minimal alterations, just a few seats removed for gambling machines. Maybe due to the proximity of the Coliseum in Green Lanes, which had been on bingo since 1961, bingo did not flourish, and films resumed on 15th February 1964. It was now known as the Curzon, and opened with a popular Norman Wisdom film *A Stitch in Time* showing in the now 500 seat auditorium.

It continued to operate under several owners, but good quality films became harder to book especially after the nearby Ritz was divided into 3 cinemas in 1977. By 1980, the Curzon had become rather seedy and was showing a regular programme of double sex films- relieved by Asian films on Sundays. This did not find favour with the licensing authority – then the Greater London Council – who tried to withdraw the Curzon's cinema licence. The owner, Roche Tagliani, objected to this and the case eventually went to Wood Green Crown Court in 1986, where the cinema won the day, arguing that the films they showed had been certificated by the British Board of Film Censors so could be shown in any cinema without special conditions attached. Despite this victory, the Curzon closed in 1989.

After a short period of disuse, in 1991 it became the Quazar Laser Game Centre – slogan "Serious Fun with a Laser Gun". This involved painting the interior black, and erecting subdivisions to create "rooms". Patrons then pursued each other through the "rooms" "shooting" each other with a light gun. This craze only lasted for a couple of years, and by 1996, a local church group – Church of Destiny – had moved in, despite local opposition on the grounds of noise and parking. But the church did not stay long, and within a year had vacated.

The building then became a cinema again – opening in 1997 as the New Curzon. It was an enterprise of Mr Jitu Ravall, who ran a similar cinema in Birmingham, and it showed exclusively Asian – or "Bollywood" – films. The cinema's original ceiling was beyond economic repair, so a flat false ceiling was erected beneath it, and a large new screen erected in front of the old one. Seating capacity was reduced to a comfortable 498 (just over half the capacity the cinema had on opening in 1910).

The reborn cinema proved popular, and its 90th year was celebrated on April 16th 2000 by a showing of the 1957 film *The Smallest Show on Earth* starring Peter Sellars and Margaret Rutherford. This has as its storyline the struggle to operate a small run-down cinema.

But from August 2000, the New Curzon faced severe

competition when a new 12-screen Cineworld complex opened in Wood Green High Road. This had regular showings of "Bollywood" films and could obtain the latest films before the New Curzon could get them. After struggling for over two years, the New Curzon closed in January 2003.

The Premier in 2009 as the Liberty Church   (Peter Staveley)

It was soon occupied by another church group – Liberty Church – who have proved more permanent residents. The art-deco front has been refurbished and remains an impressive sight, whilst the auditorium has retained the false ceiling. As the building celebrates its centenary, it is good to know that it is still standing and in regular use.

ELECTRIC COLISEUM / COLISEUM

10 Salisbury Promenade ("Salisbury Corner"), Green Lanes, Harringay, N8 0AX (at corner of St. Ann's Road)

Opened 16th November 1910. Closed 3rd June 1961.
Became a bingo club, then a furniture warehouse.
Demolished 1999, flats and shops now on the site.

This early cinema was built by Electric Coliseums Ltd opposite the imposing Salisbury Hotel and had an impressive decorative façade to attract the passing traveller along Green Lanes. The architectural design was by O.R. Dawes, and the *Bioscope Magazine* describes the interior as having "lounge-chairs, gold-framed, with crimson plush, the colour scheme is cream-green and gold. The floor is covered by Wilton pile carpet in one piece. There is a large gallery and seating for 1500 persons." In fact, the actual seating capacity was rather less, around 641, seated in stalls and a shallow balcony, which had a decorated front. A small stage could be used for variety acts. In 1913, a 2-manual 17-stop straight organ was installed. This was purchased second-hand from a church, and was believed to be made by Jones of Holloway, or by Rest-Cartwright. The first organist was Ewart Lyne

In the 1920s, an assistant organist at matinee performances was Harry Bidgood (1894-1957) who later became a leading musical director, supervising some 15 feature films between 1939 and 1946. These included several of George Formby's films, such as *Bell-Bottom George*, and also *We'll Meet Again* made in 1943 and starring Vera Lynn. In the early 1930s, under the name Primo Scala, he led a successful accordion band. They often appeared at the Wood Green Empire in the 1940s and on the radio in *Music While You Work*, amongst other programmes, into the 1950s.

On an adjacent site to the north a dance hall opened shortly after the cinema, with its own entrance on Green Lanes.

Around 1930, the cinema was modified for talking films and adopted the name "Coliseum" to reflect the modern sound age! The organ fell silent, but was not removed, being hidden behind a false screen erected in front of the original stage. Around this time, the elaborate street façade was simplified to try and give a more up-to-date appearance. The cinema was owned by a Mr & Mrs Vennard, but in 1937, they went broke and

Green Lanes Harringay in 1912
showing the Coliseum Cinema in the
centre distance at the corner of St
Ann's Road. The adjacent dance hall
has yet to be built.

*(Bruce Castle Museum (Haringey
Culture, Libraries and Learning))*

(Above)
Interior of the Coliseum after its conversion to a bingo club in 1961.

(Cinema Theatre Association Archive / John D Sharp)

CINES

ANTONY & CLEOPATRA

ELECTRIC COLISEUM, *Salisbury Corner, Green Lanes, Harringay.*

Commencing MONDAY, FEBRUARY 9th. Seven Days Only.

Performances Daily, 2.45, 6.45 & 8.45.

SUNDAY, FEBRUARY 15th, at 6 & 8.

(Left)
A programme cover of 1914 from the Electric Coliseum, Harringay. Probably a standard cover provided by the film renters, overprinted with the Coliseum's details.

(Courtesy of Special Collections, University of Exeter)

33

returned to their native Ireland, selling the building to J.Dent of Universal Amusements. By 1939, the owners were Bijou Ltd. The Coliseum continued to be popular until the general decline in cinema attendance started, and it closed in 1961 with the films *Who Was That Lady* starring Tony Curtis and *Buchanan Rides Alone* with Randolph Scott.

It became a bingo club, still called the Coliseum. From photographs, the conversion seems to have been minimal, retaining the cinema seats in stalls and balcony, with a few rows removed at the rear for gaming machines.

The much-simplified exterior of the Coliseum as a Bingo Club, pictured in the 1970s.
(Cinema Theatre Association Archive)

Throughout all these years, the organ had remained boarded up behind the false stage. It was "discovered" by John A Berry, who wrote about it in the *Hornsey Journal* of September

21st 1979. Shortly afterwards, the bingo club closed and the building was acquired by the Protopapas family for conversion to a warehouse for their adjoining furniture shop.

Through the intervention of cinema organist Doug Sharp, the organ was removed and transferred to Picardy School at Belvedere, Kent where it formed an organ-building project for the pupils under the leadership of Alec Hithersay. Unfortunately, the project was never completed, and the organ was eventually donated to a local history museum at Welling, Kent in 1983 where it remains in store.

The Coliseum's new life as a warehouse lasted until the late 1980s, and it then stood empty and decaying until 1999 when it was demolished. Flats and shops now occupy the site.

The adjacent dance hall is now a club and bar. In the 1980s it was known as Bolts, catering mainly for a gay audience. Amongst the well-known performers who made their early appearances there were the Weather Girls and the singer George Michael, as part of the pop duo Wham!

Alan Clark who lives in London, recalls the Coliseum:
"I probably first visited in 1947, aged 11 or 12. I remember a fat gentleman (manager or possibly owner) standing outside and cajoling children to see the show (wouldn't be allowed today). It was a small screen. It was a duty of the usherettes to ensure seats were vacated at the end of the programme. (A source of contention- 'you've seen it- get out' 'No I haven't – I've just come in') Initially the price was sixpence (2 1/2p). I think it went up to tenpence (4p) and a shilling (5p) in later years, upstairs (the circle) was probably more – don't think I ever went. Very popular because it was within walking distance of anyone living in Harringay. There were a couple of downsides- shouts, whistles and boos when the film broke- usually at least once per performance. Plus the circle was upheld by two metal supports approximately 4-inches in diameter which obscured the view of the audience behind!

I occasionally visited the Regal in Frobisher Road by Ducketts Common. This cinema seemed unusual because it had no circle."

GRAND PICTURE PALACE / NEW CLARENCE / REGENT

139 Turnpike Lane, Hornsey, N8 0EA

Opened 5th August 1911. Closed 1934.
Became a car repair workshop, later demolished for road-widening scheme.

This cinema was built on a vacant site at the western corner of Wightman Road and Turnpike Lane and was owned by Robert C Buchanan, trading as Cecil Cinemas. Buchanan had already opened the Picture House in nearby Tottenham Lane earlier in the year. At Turnpike Lane, the building had around 700 seats according to the Bioscope Directory. By 1914, the owners had become Adelphi Picture Theatres – this may have been the Cecil Cinemas company renamed.

In 1929, the cinema was equipped for sound films – the "Edibell" system was installed – and was renamed the New Clarence. By 1933, the name had changed again to the Regent. But the cinema closed soon after this and in 1934, became a car body repair workshop, eventually owned by the CSM Company.

The former Grand / Clarence / New Regent in Turnpike Lane, shortly before demolition in 1970.

(Kevin Wheelan)

In the 1970s, the premises were demolished, together with all the surrounding property, in order to widen Wightman Road. Due to renumbering, the present property at 139, Turnpike Lane is not in the same location as the cinema.

RITZ / ABC / CANNON / CORONET

9, Turnpike Parade, Green Lanes, N15 3EA

*Opened 30th December 1935. Closed 25th March 1999.
Demolished. Site of auditorium now part of bus station.
Site of foyer block now flower shop.*

The Ritz was conceived and designed by Major W.J. King who built a string of cinemas, nearly always called Ritz, in North and West London (other examples locally were at Potters Bar, now demolished, and in Bowes Road, New Southgate which survives as a Jehovah's Witness meeting hall). These were often built as speculative ventures, then an operator was signed up just before completion or soon afterwards. In the case of this Ritz – normally referred to as the Ritz, Turnpike Lane, but sometimes the Ritz Harringay – ABC was the operator from opening day. ABC-Associated British Cinemas – was the largest of the major cinema chains in the 1930s, owning at their peak some 600 cinemas throughout the UK.

The Ritz was adjacent to Turnpike Lane Underground Station, which had opened 3 years previously, in 1932. It was attached to a row of shops, the whole site being leased from London Transport (LPTB). This prominent position meant that the cinema could cater for homeward bound commuters and local residents alike, and was most popular as a result. A tea lounge with seating for 50 persons was located above the foyer, but this had closed by the 1950s and was converted to office space. An adjacent restaurant in Turnpike Parade was named "The Ritz Grill" but presumably no-one got it confused with the famous Ritz in Piccadilly.

The entrance and foyer were somewhat restricted, but they led to a spacious auditorium, with seating for 1269 in the stalls and 569 in the wide circle which had only a small overhang above the stalls. There were attractive art-deco style decorations on the walls, and wide promenades along the rear of the stalls and balcony.

The Ritz, Harringay / Turnpike Lane, pictured in 1946.
(Cinema Theatre Association Archive)

The fine interior of the Ritz, Harringay, shortly after opening.
(Cinema Theatre Association Archive)

The opening film programme consisted of a Mickey Mouse cartoon, a *Pathe Super Sound Gazette*, and two films: *Sing me a Love Song* featuring Ricardo Cortez and Dorothy Page, and *China Seas* starring Clark Gable and Jean Harlow.

The Ritz was often chosen to present special events – for example, in 1961 the World Premiere of the Children's Film Foundation (CFF) film *The Monster of Highgate Ponds.* (The CFF had been founded to provide suitable film material for children's matinees, Saturday shows, etc). Later, in 1969, the cinema was host to the first "Chiffy" awards presented to the best CFF film voted for by the 100,000 ABC "Minors" – the children's cinema club operated by the chain. The Ritz had a thriving Minors club.

The Ritz, Harringay renamed as the ABC, pictured in 1963. *(Dusashenka collection)*

In 1961, the name "Ritz" was dropped in favour of plain "ABC" – the same fate happened to many other ABC-operated cinemas, including the one at Muswell Hill. The cinema was later equipped with the giant screen "Todd AO" 70mm process (70mm film is double the size of that normally used and has six magnetic stereo soundtracks) and enjoyed extended runs of such films as *Doctor Zhivago* and *Where Eagles Dare* as well as one-day revivals of 70mm classics.

But attendances were still declining, so in 1977, the cinema underwent the "tripling" treatment and was subdivided into three smaller cinemas. A wall was built just ahead of the circle front, and then the lower area was divided into two. The circle area was extended forward slightly, with a new screen erected well forward of the original. The resulting seating figures were 625 in the former circle area, now called screen 1, and 417 and 316 seats in the two "minis", screens 2 and 3, under the circle. Any remaining traces of 1930s decoration disappeared around this time and the resulting auditoria were rather plain and bland.

In 1986, the Cannon group took control of the ABC cinema chain, and the cinema was renamed Cannon. This lasted only until 1988 when the cinema was acquired by the independent Coronet chain, and renamed Coronet.

This was to last only a further 11 years, because London Transport wished to extend the adjacent bus station, and terminated the cinema's lease which was not due to expire until 2034. So the cinema closed on 25th March 1999 and was demolished in July of that year. The final films shown were *Patch Adams* starring Robin Williams in the main screen and *This Years Love* and *Urban Legend* in the two smaller screens. It was not until 2000 that the first of Wood Green's multiplex cinemas opened, so for just over a year, the only mainstream cinema entertainment available in the whole of Haringey was at the Odeon Muswell Hill.

The site of the auditorium is now an open parking area as part of the bus station, and a new building was erected on the site of the cinema's foyer, currently occupied by a flower shop.

Clive Brown, who now lives in High Wycombe, was a projectionist at the Ritz from 1948 to 1961:
"I started as a trainee, the week I started we were playing

'Treasures of the Sierra Madre' with Humphrey Bogart. To this day, I can still remember the music score and the excitement of this wonderful new world to me. The Ritz was a wonderful theatre, and all the staff, including the various managers I worked under, were like a big family. I left for National Service in 1950, as a third operator, and returned in 1954 as a second operator. My years with ABC at the Ritz were the happiest of my working life."

Frank Snart, who now lives in Dorset, started as a trainee manager at the ABC in 1970:
"After three months I was promoted to Grade D Assistant Manager (there being four grades- ABCD- A being the top grade) which meant I was authorised to be left in charge of the premises. In 1973, the area manager conned me into being Assistant at Stoke Newington, which I hated, so I left to become manager of the Strand Cinema in Bideford, Devon. It rained every day, so over the winter I came back to Turnpike Lane in 1974. It was always a busy cinema- we use to joke that you could put on somebody's holiday slides and people would still come! The 70mm specials were always popular, and 'Dr Zhivago' particularly so.

One amusing incident I recall was during a run of the film 'Little Big Man' starring Dustin Hoffman in 1970. Towards the end of the film there is a scene featuring heavy rainfall, and at that point the large water tank above the screen decided to spring a leak, with water running down the screen. The projectionist and I didn't notice it at first, then when the rain scene finished, we thought it was a bad scratch on the film. Only when the film ended, and the scratch continued to show, did we realise it was something more serious."

Liz Ixer, who lives in Harringay, remembers the Coronet days:
"I went here in its dying days. My friends liked it because you could smoke in it. There seemed to be only one member of staff, a burly chap who sold tickets, then dashed to the other side of the foyer and sold you ice cream as well as chucking out unruly types. It was a little like a cinema in a sitcom. I went to see 'Star Wars' one evening when it came out again and the manager put up the house lights and started cleaning – 10 minutes before the end of the film!"

Horŋsey, Crouçh Eŋd aŋd Highgate

PICTURE HOUSE / PERFECT / PLAZA

165 Tottenham Lane, Crouch End, N8 9BT

Opened 15th April 1911. Closed 28th September 1940.
Damaged by enemy action and later demolished.
Offices are now on the site.

This was the first purpose-built cinema in the Hornsey and Crouch End area – until it was built residents had been able to see films in the National Hall in Hornsey High Street, the Assembly Rooms in Middle Lane and occasionally at the Hippodrome.

The Picture House was built in part of the grounds of Lightcliffe House. The *Hornsey Journal* of April 14th 1911 describes the new building as having "a handsome pillared frontage of some 50 ft. Upper elevation tastefully carved in stone. Interior is prettily designed, it's seating and features are luxurious and well-arranged. Accommodation for afternoon tea and light refreshments". There were around 600 seats.

The proprietor was Robert C. Buchanan, trading as Cecil Cinemas – who also operated the nearby Grand Cinema in Turnpike Lane and a cinema in Tottenham also called The Grand. By 1914, the owners were Adelphi Pictures Ltd, and press advertisements offered "illuminated gardens"- presumably in the areas around the cinema building. The *Hornsey Journal* stated that "in fine weather, the pictures could be moved outdoors" – it is not clear how this could be achieved without some difficulty!

The cinema closed around the time of the outbreak of World War One – the last press advertisements appeared on July 31st 1914. It was not uncommon for cinemas to close around this period – they found it difficult to obtain new films and also sufficient staff to operate the building.

The building re-opened on March 29th 1919, with a new name – the Perfect Picture House. The Mayor of Hornsey was present at the opening, and he returned a week later for a special charity film show.

In December 1929, the cinema was wired for sound films and renamed again, as the Plaza. The owner was now Mr Baron Sampson. In 1935, there was some modernisation with a new and larger screen. In August 1936 it closed for 2 weeks for re-seating and redecoration, and upon reopening on September 11th 1936, it was advertised as "North London's Film Repertory Cinema". This meant that it generally didn't show the latest films, but re-releases of older titles and patrons were invited to suggest films that they wanted to see. This programming change may have been due to difficulties in obtaining the current new release films because of the proximity of the Gaumont – run Hippodrome a few yards away, and also from December 1935 the new ABC-operated Ritz at Turnpike Lane Station.

The *Hornsey Journal* of 27th September 1940 carried the announcement that the Plaza was "Closing for the time being, due to falling off of attendances due to air raids. The management trust to have a renewal of your patronage when brighter times allow of re-opening. Keep Smiling – see you again soon". The date of the closing night was not mentioned, but was likely to have been 28th September 1940 when the main feature of the show was *The Great Victor Herbert* starring Allan Jones and Mary Martin together with a revival of *Fra Diavolo* featuring Laurel and Hardy.

Sadly the Plaza never re-opened, for on the night of November 1st 1940, a bomb exploded outside in Tottenham Lane and badly damaged the building. 8 people were killed in that air raid, mainly motorists and pedestrians, including 1 person who had been sheltering on the steps of the closed cinema. It is maybe fortunate that the cinema was closed, as the casualty rate would probably have been higher.

The damaged building was cemented over and an emergency water supply tank was erected amongst the ruins. The Journal of 17th April 1942 says that the screen was left in place, reflecting eerily on the water's surface.

After the war, a light engineering works was erected on the site in the 1950s, but in the 1960s a block of offices was built-Rosebery House – currently occupied by the building company of Suman Brothers.

HIPPODROME

31 Topsfield Parade, Tottenham Lane, Crouch End, N8 8PT

Opened (as full-time cinema) 4th August 1913. Closed 28th April 1942, due to fire damage. Became a dance studio, then a warehouse. Auditorium demolished, frontage remains, site of auditorium now a health club/gym.

This building opened as a live theatre, the Queen's Opera House, on 27th July 1897. It had originally been planned by the developer of Topsfield Parade, James Edmondson, to be a public hall or "Athenaeum" but before completion, the plans had been modified by the noted theatre architect Frank Matcham, and the resultant theatre was operated by two theatre proprietors, H.H. Morrell and Frederick Mouillot. The capacity was somewhat small – around 1,200 seats – and there was only one balcony and no space for an upper gallery, because incorporated in the building were a smaller hall and other rooms which could be hired. The theatre's name changed to Crouch End Opera House by the end of 1897 and then, after a period of closure due to a fire in 1904, it became Crouch End Hippodrome in 1906.

Crouch End Hippodrome photographed in 1945, closed after a fire in 1942. It never re-opened. *(Allen Eyles collection)*

Films were shown, between the plays and variety, from as early as 1910, when to comply with the new Cinematograph Act, a projection room was constructed, to the plans of noted local architect John Farrer, above the rear of the circle. Variety continued to be the main attraction, but had declined in popularity and the theatre closed on 15th February 1913 to be converted to a full-time cinema. The proprietors, Crouch End Playhouse Ltd, engaged architect Edward A. Stone, of the firm Norfolk and Prior, to carry out the alterations. The main work involved was to construct a larger projection box, at the rear of the circle, and a rewind room, where the films were rewound after showing. Seating capacity was reduced slightly to 1,000 seats. The re-opening film on 4th August 1913 was *Quo Vadis?* which, at 9-reels and around 120 minutes long, is often claimed to be the first full-length feature film ever produced. It was accompanied by a full orchestra and there was also a performance by a concert party at each show.

There were still occasional live shows, including some by the local amateur group, Crouch End Operatic and Dramatic Society. In 1927 they celebrated the 30th anniversary of the building by staging *The Geisha* the production which had opened the theatre in 1897.

By 1928 the Hippodrome was operated by General Theatre Corporation, and in April that year this circuit was acquired by the growing Gaumont British Picture Corporation. When sound films arrived, there were some alterations in 1929 and 1930 by the Gaumont house architect, W. E. Trent (who would later design the Gaumont Palace at Wood Green).

The cinema was never renamed Gaumont as others on the circuit were, but continued as the Hippodrome until, in the early hours of April 29th 1942, there was a serious fire, largely confined to the roof. The cinema closed, although the meeting rooms and dance hall at the front of the building were unaffected. The final films shown on the previous evening had been *Back Room Boy* with Arthur Askey and *Mob Town*. A few days beforehand, the film showing had been the appropriately-named *Hot Spot* starring Betty Grable!

The cinema never re-opened – plans were drawn up by W. E. Trent in 1945, and revised in 1946, for rebuilding as a cinema with 1,000 seats on a single stadium-like floor. But the Middlesex County Council did not approve the plans, commenting on the application that they "cannot agree to erection of a new cinema on the grounds that the said site fails materially to conform to the Council's regulations covering sites for this class of building". Maybe they considered the site was too small and there was too much surrounding residential property. The plans were not re-presented and the cinema idea was dropped.

The building was eventually repaired and became dance studios from 1948, then a storage warehouse by the 1950s. Later, the mail-order company Grattan used it as their warehouse and offices, concealing the original frontage with dark brown glass cladding, destroying the original symmetry of Topsfield Parade. They eventually demolished the auditorium and rebuilt it as a warehouse. After they moved out in the early 2000s, the building became a health club and gym, and it remains so, currently operated by Virgin Leisure. The cladding has thankfully been removed from the frontage, and a partial restoration in keeping with the original design has been carried out.

Stanley Smith, writing in the *CTA Bulletin* in 2001, recalls:
"I remember visiting the Hippodrome as a child during the 1930s. My mother took me to matinees during the school holidays and I can still recall the plush carpeting and the exotic smell on entering the vestibule. When buying a ticket, the question was always asked "Will you require tea and biscuits in the interval?" Coming from a working class background with a father on short time, the answer was always a polite refusal. The discreet clinking of cups and saucers just prior to the interval was a useful guide to the ending of a sometimes boring first feature. Occasionally I would be taken to an evening performance at the dear old "Hip". Mother and I would meet dad who had come straight from work and she would hand him his sandwiches wrapped in greaseproof paper. A great deal of skill was required unwrapping them without making undue noise."

Other places in the area where films were shown:

ASSEMBLY ROOMS *(Crouch End)*

15 The Pavement, Middle Lane, Crouch End, N8 8PL
(present-day address is 2-6 Middle Lane)

This building was constructed around 1900 and used for various meetings and functions, including those of the Salvation Army who used the hall from 1907. The *Bioscope* magazine of 24th March 1910 announced that "Crouch End is to have a new Bioscope, where the Assembly Rooms are to be operated by Mr Goodridge". But the management soon changed, as the *Hornsey Journal* of May 6th 1910 announces the "Crouch End Electric Family Theatre at the Assembly Rooms. The Happy Rendezvous for the Leisure Hour, under the new management a really finished and refined programme is submitted – the World's Best Pictures. A Continuous Entertainment from 6.30 p.m." The *Bioscope* magazine's reporter visited on 12th May and commented that "there were seats for around 250 but it was not well patronised".

The operators were Bijou Picture Theatres Ltd, who also operated a cinema at Camberwell, but by the end of 1910 they had ceased trading. The *Hornsey Journal* of March 3rd 1911 advertises "The New Picture Palace" at the Assembly Rooms, proprietor George Fry. This venture lasted until around 1914, when no doubt the superior comfort of the almost adjacent Crouch End Hippodrome, which was by then a full-time cinema, proved more popular.

The Assembly Rooms became a factory around 1920-Assembly Works, owned at first by Fraser and Glass, metal stampers and moulders- but in the 1970s the building was demolished for an office block. In 2010, the building is being redeveloped again as a mixed residential and office building.

NATIONAL HALL

31-33 High Street, Hornsey, N8 7QB

This hall was built in 1888 as the National Hall & Constitutional Club, by architect John Farrer. It contained several function rooms and a large hall seating around 500. In 1910, this space became a full-time cinema, operated by Biograph Theatres Ltd, who had a chain of 9 cinemas, in areas including Kilburn, Peckham and Ilford. The National Hall Cinema is last mentioned in the *Kinematograph Year Book* of 1916 so is likely to have ceased being a cinema around this time. (In an article in *HHS Bulletin* No 35, Arthur Batterbury recalls visiting in 1915 and paying one penny to see Tom Mix – who was the first really popular star of cowboy films).

The Hall reverted to being a venue for various functions, and today is the Magic Flute Banqueting Suite, popular for wedding receptions.

HORNSEY PALACE / STAR

335 Hornsey Road, Hornsey Rise, N19 4HF

The former entrance to the Hornsey Palace / Star amongst a row of houses, taken in 1970 just before demolition.

(Kevin Wheelan)

Located just over the Islington border, this small cinema would have attracted patrons from the Hornsey Rise corner of Haringey. A project of Islington Cinemas Ltd, it opened in August 1911, and was an ingenious conversion by architects Lawrence & Clark, of a terraced house to form the entrance foyer. Another house along the street providing the emergency exit, and an auditorium for around 500 people was erected in the back garden area between the two. The houses in between must have had an uninspiring view from their back windows! It was renamed the Star in 1922, and was adapted for sound in 1930, but closed around 1937. It was used as a warehouse for many years, but was demolished in the 1970s when the area was comprehensively redeveloped, and housing covers the site today.

ELECTRIC PALACE / PALACE

17, Highgate Hill, Archway, N19 5NA

The Electric Palace on Highgate Hill photographed in 1922.

(Islington Local History Centre)

Although a cinema was never built in Highgate or Highgate Village, people from these areas could descend Highgate Hill to visit this cinema, located just over the Islington boundary, adjacent to the Underground station (first known as Highgate and later as Archway). The Cinema opened in December 1912 and was owned by Electric Palaces Ltd. The architect was Gilbert W Booth who produced a striking exterior, with a large arched entrance, illuminated at night by rows of electric lights. Inside there were 774 seats on a single floor, and the silent films were accompanied by the Palace Orchestra. By 1914 the cinema had been acquired by the Sidney Bacon circuit, and then passed to Union Cinemas, a large national chain, by 1932. This chain was acquired by the larger ABC circuit in 1937. The cinema was renamed the Palace in 1954, but closed on April 12th 1958 with the appropriately-named film *Sayonara* starring Marlon Brando. Its demise may have been hastened by the opening of the much more luxurious Odeon in Junction Road in 1955. The Palace was demolished and the site was redeveloped as part of the large Archway office development.

ODEON *(Highgate, also in Islington and not illustrated)*

52 Junction Road (cnr Bickerton Road), Archway, N19 5XP

This large cinema, with 1774 seats, had been started before the Second World War, and the unfinished building was requisitioned and used for the storage of furniture. There was a considerable delay in restarting the building work after the War, and the cinema finally opened on 19th December 1955 with the film An Alligator Named Daisy starring Donald Sinden and Diana Dors. The architects were T.P. Bennett & Sons, responsible for several post-war Odeon cinemas. The Odeon was to be open for just over 17 years, with closure on 6th January 1973 with the films *Carry on Abroad* and *East Side West Side*. The building was demolished, and a block of flats, Ash Court, was built, but part of the Odeon's exterior wall can still be seen fronting Junction Road.

/\\uswell Hill

MUSWELL HILL ELECTRIC THEATRE / SUMMERLAND CINEMA

Summerland Gardens, Muswell Hill , N10 3PQ

Opened 8th April 1912. (See photo on front cover)
Closed 11th February 1938.
Demolished and car park for Summerland Grange flats is on site.

This was the first purpose-built cinema in Muswell Hill, built on part of the grounds of a demolished mansion called Summerlands. Most of the grounds had been developed by Thomas Finnane, who built a block of mansion flats and shops facing Muswell Hill Broadway in 1904. The remainder of the site was steep and proved difficult to develop for houses, so became a form of pleasure grounds, with coloured lanterns and outdoor musical performances.

Cinemas were relatively late in coming to Muswell Hill, compared with other districts of London where some had been established as early as 1907. This was due to local opposition to this modern attraction, which had been satirised in the trade press – the *Bioscope Newsletter* – in 1909, where they had nicknamed the suburb "Muswell Ill".

The cinema within the pleasure grounds was opened on Easter Monday 1912, by the Muswell Hill Electric Theatre Company. It utilised the natural steepness of the landscape to provide the sloping rake needed for the seating area without the need for expensive excavation. The *Hornsey Journal* stated that "the new building has seats for several hundred, and a private box seating nine. The façade is incomplete". Shows, lasting 2 hours, were advertised from 2.00 p.m. to 10.00 p.m. except Sundays, the price of admission to the cinema and gardens was 6d (2^1/2p) or to the cinema only, 3d (1^1/2p). The private box cost 10s 6d (52^1/2p). In his book "The Growth of Muswell Hill", Jack Whitehead describes the building as "like a theatre at the end of a seaside pier"!

A surviving programme from September 1913 mentions the films *The Drummer of the Eighth*, an American Civil war drama, and *His Life for His Emperor*, a film about Napoleon produced by the Vitagraph Company. A forthcoming attraction was *The Battle of Waterloo*.

The cinema seems to have been successful, and in the 1918 Kinematograph Yearbook it is stated that there were 500 seats. In 1919, the original owners sold the theatre to S. Midick, and in 1920 the cinema was renamed Summerland Cinema under new owner C. Boss. The *Kine Weekly* of July 15th 1920 reported that "the gardens behind the cinema had opened as an al-fresco concert area, illuminated by gas fairy-lamps. On wet evenings, performances are held in the kinema".

In 1925, Summerland was acquired by Arthur Ferriss who already operated the Athenaeum cinema nearby in Fortis Green Road. He was the managing director, later the owner, of Home Counties Theatres Ltd, which also operated the Coliseum Cinema at East Finchley, still open today as the Phoenix. Arthur Ferriss had an interesting early career as a "character comedian" at music halls, including appearances at Wood Green Empire in 1912.

Summerland continued to prosper until 1935 when a cloud appeared on the horizon with the news that two large cinema chains ABC and Odeon – had acquired sites in Muswell Hill to build super-cinemas. The *Hornsey Journal* had many reports of the resulting "cinema wars". ABC chose the site of the Green Man garage on Muswell Hill itself – the site almost backed on to the Summerland Gardens – whilst Odeon at first favoured a site at the junction of Colney Hatch Lane and Muswell Avenue. This was doubly unfortunate for Arthur Ferriss – his house was in Muswell Avenue and would be demolished for the new Odeon. In the event, Odeon were unable to acquire all the property they needed and instead built at Fortis Green Road.

The files of Middlesex County Council contain many

letters of protest from Ferriss claiming that his livelihood would be ruined by the new cinemas. He announced that Summerland would be developed into a super-cinema to rival the others, and plans were drawn up by local architect George Hastings, which were approved by Hornsey Council in June 1935, but the rebuilding was never carried out. Ferriss's protests came to nothing and the new cinemas went ahead, the Odeon opening in September 1936 and the ABC-operated Ritz followed in December.

At the time of the opening of the Odeon, Arthur Ferriss told the *Hornsey Journal* that "Summerland would not be closing, it will close for one week for alterations and reseating". The 1936 Kine Year Book gives the seating capacity as 680.

But Summerland could not compete for long with the superior comforts of the new cinemas, and closed just over a year later in February 1938. It was offered for sale by auction on February 4th, but the bids were not high enough. The final films on 11th February were *The Edge of the Word* starring Belle Christall and Niall McGuiness, with *Up For The Derby* starring Sydney Howard.

The building remained shuttered and disused until 1939, when a plan was announced in the Journal to make the building a second home for the Intimate Theatre, a well-established repertory company whose main base was in Palmers Green. Plans were drawn up in March 1939 by noted cinema and theatre architect Leslie Kemp, which included a small extension to the original building and seats for 550 people. The plans were approved in June 1939, and some work began on the building, but the start of the war stopped this, and the planning application was withdrawn in May 1941. After the war the plans were not revived.

The building became derelict and was damaged by fire, and lingered on into the 1950s – a former local resident, Colin Bednarz, remembers playing amongst the ruins as a child. Eventually, the site was redeveloped as a block of flats, called Summerland Grange, completed in 1959, but the site of the cinema itself is largely occupied by the car park for the flats.

Sheila Lahr, who grew up in Wilton Road, Muswell Hill, recalls in her autobiography *Yealm*:
"Of the Summerland, I seem to have a clear picture of a plain,

square building, the exterior cement-washed yellow or beige. In front of the screen and on the floor are tubs of plants and flowers, probably artificial. I am almost sure that it was at the Summerland that I watched a Laurel and Hardy film in which a piano falls down a flight of steps, taking one of the actors with it. I see no humour in this episode, for me it's a terrible and painful accident, and I scream so loudly that the manager asks my mother to leave and take me with her!

My mother goes so often to the cinema that she is known to the cashiers and so these young women never charge for me or my sister, the three of us going in for 6d. My mother is much put out when the Odeon and the Ritz are built and operate on a much more impersonal basis." (The film Sheila refers to is The Music Box made in 1932).

THE ATHENAEUM PICTURE PLAYHOUSE / ATHENAEUM CINEMA

12 Fortis Green Road, Muswell Hill, N10 3HN

Opened (for films) 23rd November 1918.
Closed 14th November 1936.
Became a dance-hall, then later demolished.
Sainsbury's supermarket is now on the site.

This building was constructed in 1900 by developer James Edmondson to serve as a focal point for the social activities of Muswell Hill. The elegant classical building, with two domed towers, contained a large hall seating 466, with a balcony, and a smaller hall seating 200, as well as several other smaller function rooms. It was the scene for dances, concerts, lectures and meetings, including the debating society known as the Muswell Hill Parliament.

The Athenaeum, Muswell Hill in use as a cinema in the 1920s. Notice the site on the left where the Odeon would later be constructed. (Crown Copyright: The National Archives).

In 1918 the larger hall was leased out and became a full-time cinema, operated by a company called Essandelle Ltd- the name probably formed from the two initials of the owners. There were several letters of protest in the Muswell Hill Record about this, claiming that Muswell Hill would be losing an important social amenity to "the picture people". The paper, in their editorial, hoped that the hall, would be "restored to other uses before too long".

The opening film on November 23rd 1918 was *The Conqueror* starring William Farnum, a Fox Picture from the USA about the founding of Texas. No copies of this film are believed to exist today. The 80-minute silent was accompanied by the Athenaeum Orchestra. Prices were 6d (2^1/2) and 1s (5p) in the stalls and 1/6d (7^1/2) upstairs in the balcony. Performances were continuous from 2.30 p.m. to 10.30 p.m.

By 1919, the lessee was James Chapman and the *Kine Year Book* gives the seating capacity as 550. Jack Whitehead, in his book "The Growth of Muswell Hill", writes "The Athenaeum had been a dance hall and when it became a cinema it was always clear that we were sitting in a converted building with high ceilings and irrelevant decoration"!

Despite this criticism, the cinema seems to have been successful and in 1923 it was acquired by Arthur Ferriss, who two years later would also acquire the other cinema in Muswell Hill, Summerland. The Athenaeum was adapted for sound films in June 1930 to the plans of local architect George Hastings, and the number of seats reduced to a more comfortable 486.

Unfortunately, in 1935, the Odeon cinema chain announced that they would be building a "super-cinema" in Muswell Hill, and their final choice of site was directly across the road from the Athenaeum. In spite of protests and petitions from local residents, and from Arthur Ferriss, the new Odeon was constructed and opened in September 1936.

At the time the Odeon opened, Ferriss was undaunted by the new competition and told the *Hornsey Journal* that "The Athenaeum would carry on as people went to see a film they liked". But this did not prove to be the case and shortly Ferriss announced that "The Athenaeum will be closing as a cinema in November and re-opening as a Palais de Dance at Christmas".

The final night was November 14th 1936 and the closing films were *Captain January* starring Shirley Temple and *Every Saturday Night* starring Jed Prouty, with June Lang as the co-star of both films.

The opening of the Palais de Dance was delayed until New Years Eve, and in early 1937 advertisements were promising "dancing, cabaret and films", but the word "films" disappeared soon after this.

The Athenaeum continued to host dances and various functions in the other rooms, including jumble sales and meetings of a Spiritualist Church, until 1966 when the building was acquired by J Sainsbury and demolished for a supermarket. This building completely upset the elegant building line of Fortis Green Road. Today the only reminder of the fine building which once housed a cinema is the cul-de-sac called Athenaeum Place.

ODEON

Fortis Green Road, Muswell Hill, N10 3HP

Opened 9th September 1936. Still open for films.
Listed Grade II*

The Odeon is considered to be one of the finest art-deco style cinemas in the UK. Behind its quite simple, unassuming façade is a spectacular entrance foyer, imposing staircases and inner foyer spaces, leading to a unique auditorium, without comparison.

The site of the Odeon was a terrace of houses built sometime between 1860 and 1880. Seven of the nine houses were demolished (the two which remained are still to be seen to the south west of the cinema).the entrance to the Odeon was planned to be on the corner with Muswell Hill Road, facing St James Church with flats and shops included in the scheme each side of the entrance.

The Odeon Muswell Hill, pictured in opening week 1936. Notice that the shops and flats to the left are still to be finished. *(Reproduced by permission of English Heritage.NMR)*

There was considerable objection to the proposed cinema, with many letters of protest in 1935 from local residents to both the *Hornsey Journal* and Middlesex County Council, who had to grant the entertainment licence. Two petitions were raised, the most important one being from the Church. They were concerned that having a super-cinema opposite their entrance would not be in keeping with their activities, and they were worried about increased car parking outside the church, particularly on a Sunday evening. Although the Athenaeum opposite had been showing films for many years, the Church considered that this was small and only attracted local trade.

Odeon Cinemas arranged for the architect of the proposed cinema, George Coles, to meet with the vicar, Rev. Dunn, in July 1935 and discuss alterations to the plans. The *Hornsey Journal* reported that the "meeting was cordial but the Church authorities were adamant that they did not want a cinema built there at all". George Coles was reported to be equally adamant that a cinema would be built there whatever it took to achieve it,

Odeon Muswell Hill exterior in 1955, advertising Richard III.   *(Odeon Cavalcade)*

and pointed out that "nothing would stop the expansion of Muswell Hill, and that it was better to have a well-designed building opposite than an ugly omnibus station or garage"! Eventually, Coles produced an alternative plan which moved the cinema entrance away from the corner to the end of the block in Fortis Green Road, and set it further back from the road. The shops and flats were moved to the other end, carefully hiding the cinema entrance completely from the church and the "Odeon" name was to be discreetly positioned on the entrance canopy rather than at the top of the building as would be more usual. The plans were approved by the MCC in October 1935, but Odeon also had to agree to close the Muswell Hill Road entrance to the cinema car park on Sundays.

George Coles (1884-1963) was a prolific designer of cinemas, for Odeon and other chains- other nearby local examples of his work are the Gaumont State at Kilburn and the Carlton, Islington. His clever solution at Muswell Hill retained the auditorium in the same position, and there is an almost undetectable shift of direction from the relocated entrance and foyers.

The Odeon chain had been started by Oscar Deutsch in 1930 with the Odeon at Perry Bar, Birmingham. By clever financing, the chain expanded rapidly and by the time Muswell Hill came to be constructed, there were already about 50 or so Odeons around the UK. It has remained the most well-known cinema chain to this day, even after several changes of ownership. Many of the cinemas were in a distinctive architectural style, often with towers or fin features, and generally covered by glazed, coloured tiles known as "faience". At Muswell Hill, these tiles on the frontage were cream in colour, with black tiles on the side wings. The frontage was outlined in red neon lighting.

Entering the foyer, the unsuspecting first-time visitor is surprised to see a full-height foyer with soaring art-deco style columns, of a unique design, with two staircases to right and left. The left hand one is now obscured by the pay box and confectionery counter – the paybox was originally an island feature in the centre of the foyer. On the ground floor, and at the top of the stairs, are circular lobby spaces where you subtly

The entrance foyer of the Odeon Muswell Hill in 1936 showing central paybox, later removed.
(Reproduced by permission of English Heritage. NMR)

change direction to reach the inner foyers – the upstairs orignally housed a small café, and still features a bar. Light fittings suspended from the ceiling are arranged to direct patrons with an arrow design, which was reflected in the floor design – now covered by carpeting.

The auditorium originally seated 1,827:1,217 in the stalls and 610 in the balcony. The sweeping central light feature, pointing to the screen, has been likened to a film-strip. It has also been suggested that the designs on the side walls are reminiscent of film reels and storage cans, and also that when viewed from the balcony; the complete design resembles an old-style cash register.

On opening night, the film attraction was a special pre-release showing of *Educated Evans* starring Max Miller. Oscar Deutsch was in attendance together with the Mayor of Hornsey, and several film stars including Basil Rathbone who was most famous for portraying Sherlock Holmes in many films. The Band of Her Majesty's Scots Guards were in attendance, and the *Hornsey Journal* reported that "there was dancing on the stage

The interior of the Odeon Muswell Hill in 1936.
(Reproduced by permission of English Heritage. NMR)

until midnight". The regular film programme started on the following day with *Big Brown Eyes* starring Cary Grant and Joan Bennett.

The cinema was very popular, even after the opening of the nearby Ritz later the same year, and remained so through the 1940s and 50s. At some stage – possibly during the war – most of the neon lighting on the frontage was removed and the Odeon name was later moved from the canopy to the top of the façade.

To try and fight the general decline in cinema-going which occurred in the 1970s, it was decided to subdivide the Odeon into 3 smaller auditoria in 1974. A drop-wall was inserted from the balcony front, and the front stalls ceased to be used. Two smaller cinemas were created under the balcony, served by a new projection box. From the balcony, the view of the main space was hardly affected. Later, the disused stalls space was utilised by the Projected Picture Trust, an enthusiast society dedicated to preserving old cinema projectors and equipment, to store some of their collection. Some of these items were also displayed in the foyers, but they have now all been removed to the Trust premises at Bletchley Park, Buckinghamshire.

The nearby Ritz /ABC closed in 1978, and the Odeon was left alone to serve Muswell Hill. But the decline in attendances continued, and in 1981 the Rank Organisation, who by then controlled Odeon Cinemas, announced a long list of cinema closures throughout the UK, and Muswell Hill was included, with a closure date of October 1981. Popular local opinion was that although the cinema was trading profitably, an offer had been made for the site from a supermarket chain.

There was great local opposition to this, and a petition was raised, and just before the proposed closure date, Rank changed their mind and the cinema remained open. With the encouragement of the General Manager, Brian Lee, The North London Cinema Society was formed to encourage greater public interest in the building and it arranged many special film shows, mainly on Sunday mornings and afternoons. In the 1980s, cinemas still tended to start their first show quite late on Sundays – around 4p.m. – unlike today, when they are generally in full operation by midday, so there were opportunities for such special shows earlier in the day.

The cinema was designated a Grade II listed building in 1984. In 1990, Rank proposed serious alterations to the cinema, including building a new screen in front of the existing one, and further subdividing the building to create extra auditoria. Although all alterations would be reversible, many features would be hidden from view and the fine interior would be compromised. After much local opposition, Haringey Council refused planning permission for the alterations. Rank appealed against this decision, and a public enquiry was set for August 1991, but Rank withdrew their appeal before this took place, and the plans have never been revived.

This listing was upgraded to II* in 1997. In 2002, the building underwent a major redecoration and refurbishment. The interior colour scheme was largely changed to white and dark blue, relieved by occasional splashes of orange. The main auditorium – Screen 1, the former balcony – was re-seated and re-stepped in the front part, with more luxurious seating and improved legroom, with some seats arranged in pairs like sofas-

The interior of the Odeon as it appears today.   *(Eva Branscome)*

at a premium price. The downstairs small screens were also refurbished. Current seating capacity is 436 in Screen 1, with 165 and 166 in the small screens 2 and 3 downstairs. Thus total seating is 767, compared with 1,827 at opening in 1936.

On the exterior, the Odeon name – in a revised style of lettering – was restored to its original location above the canopy-as well as at the top of the façade-and neon was returned to the outline of the building, now in blue rather than red. (See back cover).

The only drawback to this refurbishment is that the auditorium is now rather dimly lit, and the fine art-deco features are hard to pick out. But it means that the cinema remains attractive and popular, nearly 30 years after it was threatened with closure.

Dave Brown, who lives in Alexandra Park, worked at the Odeon from 1981 to 1992:

"I first became involved with the Odeon as a result of the threatened closure in 1981. Having been a regular attendee of the cinema since childhood, I had much affection for it, so I joined a local group who opposed the closure. A petition was presented to Rank, the owners, in an attempt to get them to change their mind- fortunately the cinema was reprieved. It was essential to keep the public interest in the cinema to stave off any future closure attempts, so the North London Cinema Society was formed by Brian Lee, the General Manager, to develop additional screenings for members and others at weekends.

I became heavily involved with publicity for the Society and was spending so much time at the Odeon that Brian offered me a part-time permanent job on the staff as assistant manager. I generally worked at busy times on Thursday and Friday evenings and all day on Saturdays and Sundays.

I managed to secure the help of film historian John Huntley to help with Society events – indeed he became the saviour of the Society as his film shows were immensely popular and drew large crowds.

In 1983, London Transport was celebrating the 50th anniversary of its formation, offering an opportunity to lay on a special archive film show, and I was keen to accompany this with a display of London buses in the cinema car park. And so in September we found the car park and the frontage slip road filled with buses from all over London and other parts of the country- in excess of 40 attended. At one time Fortis Green Road was blocked by line-up of buses, and one poor confused lady was heard to remark that there were all these buses but where was her 102 to Golders Green!

On 9th September 1986, the 50th anniversary of the cinema was celebrated with a special preview of the film "Ruthless People" accompanied by a showing of the newsreel from 1936 showing the opening of the Odeon, specially restored and presented by John Huntley.

I thoroughly enjoyed my ten years at the Odeon, and cannot imagine a more pleasant environment to work in. I feel privileged to have been associated with such a superb building which I always felt at home in (and still do). I left the job in 1992 because of increased commitments with my "day job" in British Transport Advertising."

RITZ / ABC

77, Muswell Hill, N10 3PG

*Opened 21st December 1936. Closed 28th January 1978.
Demolished 1980, office block on site.*

Just three months after the nearby Odeon opened its doors, Muswell Hill found it had another super-cinema, offering a further 1,991 seats each night to add to the Odeon's 1,827. But these were popular times for cinemas, and the Ritz-operated by the rival ABC chain – had no trouble finding an audience.

Built on an awkward sloping site, almost at the top of the Hill, once occupied by the Green Man Garage, the Ritz was designed by W.R. Glen, who was the chief architect of the cinemas built by ABC. They invariably had names associated

The Ritz Muswell Hill photographed soon after opening in 1936. Notice the cardboard cut-out of Fred Astaire and Ginger Rodgers by the doors.

(Cinema Theatre Association Archive)

with luxury, such as Ritz, Savoy or Regal. ABC had already opened in the borough, at Turnpike Lane, a year earlier, but that scheme had been a takeover. Here they built their own design from scratch. The exterior had a prominent tower to attract attention from the nearby Broadway- it could be argued that the Ritz had the better site of the two new cinemas, being situated on a major road from Finsbury Park and beyond, and adjacent to Muswell Hill railway station (until it closed in 1954) where many commuters arrived home in the evenings. There was a sizeable car park at the rear.

The cinema had an inviting interior, with many features in the art-deco style – there were 1,213 seats in the stalls and 778 in the circle. Unlike the nearby Odeon, there was no grand opening ceremony, the cinema simply opened for business at 2pm with the films *Sons O'Guns* starring Joe E Brown and Joan Blondell, together with Lewis Stone and Betty Grable in *Don't Turn 'em Loose.*

The interior of the Ritz Muswell Hill in 1936.   *(Dusashenka collection)*

The *Muswell Hill Record* described the interior décor as "blended colour tones of pink merging into cream and picked out with cerise and green. The seats are of a reddish hue. The circle lounge has a domed ceiling with concealed lighting and although there has been mention of it being used as a café, none is planned at present. There is space allowed for an organ but none is planned as yet".

The Ritz followed the national trend and was renamed plain "ABC" in 1962. Its popularity started to fade, along with many local cinemas, and it eventually closed on 28th January 1978. The nearby Odeon had by then been "tripled" into smaller cinemas and could offer more choice than previously, undermining the ABC's importance. The final films were *One on One* starring Robby Benson and Melanie Griffiths and *Greased Lightning* starring Richard Pryor.

The building remained empty and decaying until it was demolished in June 1980. An office block was erected on the site, occupied at first by the brewers Taylor Walker, later by the well-known pub company Wetherspoons, but now by multiple occupiers.

Ken Gay, who lives in Alexandra Park, remembers the Ritz:
"After coming to live locally in August 1954, my wife and I visited both the Odeon and the Ritz. Some cinema buildings have a sort of magic and I felt this particularly when visiting the Ritz, a fine place. For years a middle aged lady worked there as an usherette, standing in the foyer and selling the Film Review magazine. I did not know her name but she was well known to local cinemagoers. There were some great films shown- our route home was down Dukes Avenue on foot and I remember dancing and singing a bit after seeing one film, possibly 'Seven Brides for Seven Brothers'. Did some Dukes Avenue residents think this was not seemly Muswell Hill behaviour?"

Films are also shown in the area at:

PHOENIX

52 High Road, East Finchley, N2 9PJ

Although situated just over the border in the Borough of Barnet, the Phoenix is included here as many local residents of Muswell Hill visit the cinema. It is one of the oldest operating cinemas in Britain, the plans by architect S. Birdwood receiving planning permission in September 1910, although opening was delayed until 1912, as The Picturedrome. In 1925, it became The Coliseum, owned by Home Counties Theatres who also operated the Athenaeum and Summerland cinemas at Muswell Hill. They gave up in 1938 and the cinema was then renamed The Rex and rebuilt with a much more modern "art-deco" look by architects Howes and Jackman, with an interior decoration scheme by Mollo & Egan which retained the original barrel-vaulted ceiling. There was seating for 528, all on one level with no balcony.

The Phoenix in 1983.

(Phoenix Cinema Trust)

After several changes of ownership, coupled with threats of closure and demolition, followed by a change of name to The Phoenix in 1975, the cinema is now owned by the Phoenix Cinema Trust. The Trust embarked on a major renovation and restoration scheme for its centenary year. It is a Grade II listed building, much-loved by its regular audiences. Seating is now more comfortable, with a capacity of 289.

Tottenham

PEOPLE'S PALACE

Forster Road (corner of Chaplin Road), Tottenham N17 6QD

Opened September 1907. Closed June 1923.
Became light industrial unit and warehouse,
now a place of worship.

This was the first regular full-time cinema operation in the Borough. The first advertisement appeared in the *Weekly Herald* of September 4th 1907 advertising shows for the week commencing September 2nd.

The building had started life in 1885 as a meeting hall for the Blue Ribbon Gospel Temperance Movement, but this did not prosper and the building became available for letting as Forster Hall. Early showings of "Animated Photographs", including scenes of Queen Victoria's funeral, took place in March 1901, probably the first such showings in Tottenham. In July 1901, it became the People's Palace of Varieties under the directorship of John Lawson and his wife, Cissie. Following an old theatre tradition, they were actor-managers, appearing in many of the sketches themselves.

The theatre sometimes advertised as "Tottenham Palace", not to be confused with the large variety theatre which opened in 1908 on Tottenham High Road.

The People's Palace ceased to be a live theatre, and in 1907 was taken over by Walturdaw Animated Pictures as a full-time cinema. There were two shows nightly, at 7 and 9.10 p.m., and amongst the opening films were *The Gipsy's Revenge* and *Peter's Pranks* together with "Illustrated Songs". There was a matinee at 3pm on Saturdays aimed particularly at children. The

People's Palace

FORSTER ROAD, TOTTENHAM.

—— Under the Direction of the TOTTENHAM FORUM, LTD. ——

Having been appointed Manager of this, the
PIONEER PICTURE PALACE of Tottenham,

JOSEPH L. S. MOSS

late Proprietor of the THEATRE ROYAL, Edmonton, will be pleased to welcome all his old patrons
at the above Palace which has been

—— **Redecorated and Reseated** ——

AT ENORMOUS EXPENSE.

CONTINUOUS Performance, 6 to 11.

Prices from 2d. to 6d.

Children's Matinees Thursday & Saturday

1d. EACH.   DOORS OPEN AT 2.30.

Grand RE-OPENING

Saturday, April 26th, 1913,

WITH A SPECIAL PROGRAMME.

**EVERY CHILD PRESENTED WITH A PACKET OF SWEETS
& A COMIC PAPER & EVERY LADY WITH A NOVELETTE.**

O. J. HURD, Printer (T.U.), New Road, Edmonton

Advertising handbill for the re-opening of the
Peoples Palace in 1913. *(Bruce Castle
Museum (Haringey Culture, Libraries and Learning))*

Bioscope Annual for 1910 says that there were seats for 750 patrons, and despite the small size and low height of the building, there were separate charges for gallery, balcony, pit and stalls seating, implying the interior was divided into these areas.

The Walturdaw Company were engaged in many aspects of the burgeoning film industry – they were suppliers of projectors and electrical equipment, as well as stands, frames and screens, and were also rental agents for many British, Continental and American film companies. This ensured that the People's Palace received a good supply of varied films.

But despite this early success, the cinema seems to have ceased trading around August 1911 – it may have suffered from competition from the nearby Canadian Rink Cinema which had opened in 1910. But it was re-opened on April 26th 1913 under new ownership, Tottenham Forum Ltd, with Joseph L Moss as manager. The opening publicity stated that "the pioneer Picture Palace of Tottenham has been redecorated and refurbished at enormous expense". It promised that "every child will be presented with a packet of sweets and a comic paper and every lady with a novelette". Hard luck for adult gentlemen! Seating capacity was now a more comfortable 630.

The cinema continued to operate until June 1923 when

71

The former Peoples Palace in use as a light industrial unit in the 1980s.
(Cinema Theatre Association Archive)

the last advertisements appeared in the *Weekly Herald*. The owner at that time was Leslie Murray. The building became a light industrial unit, occupied for many years by the Three Hands Disinfectant Company, then later by WF electrical distributors. All traces of cinema use had been removed by the 1970s, and around 1999, the building was taken over for a place of worship by Light of the World Ministries, thus returning to the religious use it was built for in 1885.

Barbara Phillips was born in Tottenham in 1913, and recalls in her book "A Tottenham Childhood":
"Very occasionally on Saturday morning we went to a little cinema in Forster Road which we called the flea pit. For twopence each we could see a Charlie Chaplin film. They were all black and white in those days and silent, but we thought it was wonderful."

Jimmy Green, writing in "How Things Were" in 1982, recalled the People's Palace:
"I was often without the necessary one penny entrance fee, so one of us used to go into the pictures and let all the others through the exit door. We clubbed together for the money and one would go in, the rest of us would be round the back waiting. You pushed the door and in they'd all float and disappear among the crowds and congregate afterwards."

CANADIAN RINK ELECTRIC THEATRE / CANADIAN RINK CINEMA

415-419 High Road, Tottenham, N17 6QH

*Opened 19th March 1910. Closed 20th November 1924.
Became a dance hall, then nightclub. Demolished 2003,
shops and housing on site.*

Built to take advantage of two crazes for popular entertainment – roller-skating and films – the Canadian Rink consisted of two adjoining buildings, both designed by Ewen S Barr. The larger building, for skating, opened in February 1910, and the smaller Electric Theatre to the north – built right next to the Palace Theatre of Varieties – opened in March. The unusual name came from the Canadian maple wood used for the skating-rink floor. In the cinema part, there was room for around 500 people, who entered through the right-hand side of the imposing entrance, with its curved colonnade and two towers surmounted by domes.

The Canadian Rink skating rink and cinema, soon after opening in 1910. The cinema part is the low building behind the trees to the right of the main entrance. The Palace Theatre is beyond this building. Notice the "Electric Theatre" sign and the advertisement for a "Pretty Face Competition" at the skating rink.
(Bruce Castle Museum (Haringey Culture, Libraries and Learning))

The proprietors were Canadian Skating Rink and Electric Theatre Ltd, but fairly soon, they found themselves in financial difficulties, and rink and cinema had closed by June 1910. The Company went into liquidation, and a court arranged for skating, and probably films, to resume later that year under a different owner. By 1911, the business had been acquired by Goodwin and Evans of North Metropolitan Theatres Ltd, and realising that the craze for skating was passing, they decided to convert the roller-rink to a cinema.

The architect, Edward A Stone, a partner in the company of Norfolk & Prior, was engaged to transform the interior and he designed a cinema seating 1027 on the ground floor and 56 in the balcony. The smaller building which had been the Electric Theatre was then converted to a dance hall known as Canadian Hall.

The new larger Canadian Rink Cinema opened on 29 June 1911 and prospered for several years – there was no serious competition for films in the neighbourhood save the much smaller Peoples Palace nearby. By 1924, the property had been acquired by Provincial Cinematograph Theatres, who had also acquired the adjoining Tottenham Palace Theatre. They decided to transfer films into the Palace, and close the Canadian Rink Cinema, the last advertised film programme being for the week commencing 14th November 1924.

Dancing then transferred from the Canada Hall, the smaller original Electric Theatre building, to the vacated cinema and became known as Tottenham Palais de Danse, later shortened to Palais. By the 1960s, it had become the Tottenham Royal, owned by Mecca Dancing, and the well-known pop group the Dave Clark Five became one of the resident bands. Later it was renamed the Mayfair, and finally the Temple and Ozone nightclubs.

Canada Hall, the original small Electric Theatre building, was converted to a shop, for many years occupied by a draper, and then by an estate agent. Both of the buildings were demolished in 2003 and housing and shops will be found on the site today.

Ralph Berry, writing in a letter to Kevin Wheelan in 1984, recalled the Canadian Rink:

"I lived with my family from 1915 to 1917 near the Canadian Rink Cinema, my mother and father frequently took me there. A small orchestra playing from a balcony on the right side of the building accompanied the films, and there was a small organ installed as well- one of the first in the district. The centre part of the balcony was occupied by the projection box, the seating for the audience was on both sides of this room. Originally a type of double seat was installed but the licencing authority inspectors soon demanded that these seats be removed and the usual kind of single seat installed, I expect you can guess why! Later I went to work there in 1923, but I only stayed for about 5 months as I obtained a job with double the pay at a small cinema in Chingford, working as an assistant operator (projectionist).

Anyway, the Canadian Rink in its heyday from 1916 to the early 1920s was the leading cinema in the district and many people living in Edmonton who wanted to see the best and latest films travelled by tram to the Canadian Rink".

CENTRAL HALL / ROXY / MAYFAIR

64-68 High Road, South Tottenham, N15 6JU

*Opened 27th August 1910. Closed 28th January 1961.
Demolished. Loyola Hall now occupies the site.*

The Central Hall was part of a circuit of London cinemas developed by James Watt. Amongst other locations were Catford, Lewisham and Lee, all in South London, and the architect for all of them was Edward A. Stone of the company of Norfolk & Prior. Stone also designed the Stamford Hill Rink , for roller-skating, which opened just a few yards from the Central Hall, also in August 1910.

The cinema seated 100 in a small balcony, and 223 in the stalls. The building was successfully adapted for sound films in

The Central Hall, renamed as The Roxy, pictured in 1936. The queue seems to consist entirely of children, with an ice-cream cart trying to attract their custom.
(Bruce Castle Museum (Haringey Culture, Libraries and Learning))

the late 1920s, and by 1935 had changed its name to the Roxy (which was the name of a very large and lavish movie theatre in New York USA, opened in 1927, and which lent its name to countless cinemas throughout the world). It was then operated by Wardcott Cinemas Ltd, with a seating capacity of 413.

However, the cinema still had an old-fashioned look to it, and in order to compete with the much grander Regent at nearby Stamford Hill- which had opened in 1929- the Roxy closed on June 20th 1937 and was demolished, to be replaced by a new cinema, the Mayfair. The architect was Colin R. Crickmay who produced a much more modern art-deco style frontage and interior. The Mayfair opened on December 3rd 1937, with a seating capacity of 488- 336 in the stalls and 152 in the circle. The cinema was owned by Katz and Goldstine.

The Roxy was demolished and rebuilt as The Mayfair in 1937, pictured here shortly after re-opening.

(Bruce Castle Museum (Haringey Culture, Libraries and Learning))

The interior of The Mayfair.

(Bruce Castle Museum (Haringey Culture, Libraries and Learning))

The general decline in cinema attendances forced the closure of the Mayfair on 28th January 1961, and the last films shown were *The Criminal* starring Stanley Baker, and *Passionate Affair* with Christine Marquand. The building was demolished and in its place appeared Loyola Hall, a church hall for the use of St Ignatius Church which is on the opposite side of the High Road. Since the late 1990s, the hall has been used by the Brazilian-based church group, UCKG, whose UK headquarters are in another local ex-cinema building, the former Astoria at Finsbury Park – also designed by Edward A. Stone.

Kevin Wheelan, who now lives in Surrey, recalls:
"I was a pupil at St Ignatius College, which stood next to the church, from 1959 to 1965 and even in those days I was fanatical about the cinema. One of my great pleasures on alighting from the 649 trolleybus on the way to school was to look at the stills (photographs of scenes from the films) outside the Mayfair. The Jesuits, who ran St Ignatius College with a rod of iron, put all local places of entertainment out of bounds to pupils wearing school uniform. This added a sense of danger to visits to the Mayfair particularly when we were getting in to see an "X" film under age!

St. Ig's most famous "old boy" was the celebrated film director Alfred Hitchcock, who attended from 1910 to 1913, around the time the Central Hall was opening. I can imagine him looking with anticipation at the stills outside the Central Hall just as I did some 50 years later outside the Mayfair."

Joe Clark writing in a letter to Kevin Wheelan in 1984, recalled the Roxy:
"My earliest recollection of films was the Charlie Chaplin film 'Gold Rush', made in 1925, with him eating his boots, etc. Another film which made a great impression on me was 'The Patent Leather Kid' in 1927, where a disabled soldier, played by Richard Barthelmess, miraculously recovers. All the films were silent of course, but I remember being at the Roxy when as an interlude two fellows in a rowing boat started to sing audibly on film. "Good Heavens", I thought, as we went on to the next silent film, "this will never catch on". Soon after, the "talkies" arrived. But really going to the cinema wasn't all that approved of by my parents, I used to

be amazed to talk to people who went three times a week. Not too often was I permitted to go. The cinemas themselves made little impression, except the sight of queues often stretched right round the particular building especially on Friday or Saturday. One particular cinema did impress me, the Astoria at Finsbury Park – it was vast, comfortable and had twinkling stars in the ceiling."

HOTSPUR ELECTRIC THEATRE

740, High Road, Tottenham, N17 0AP (corner of Park Lane)

Opened September 1910. Closed 1921
Became a plating works, then a shop, later demolished.
The 'Spurs Shop' now occupies the site.

This cinema was converted from Fleets Auction Rooms, and the first advertisement appeared in the Weekly Herald on 30th September 1910. The proprietor was Eustace Robinson Brierley, and seats were provided for 250 patrons. The cinema was of course named after Tottenham Hotspur Football Club whose ground was adjacent.

In the 1914 *Kinematograph Year Book*, the owner was Jas Watkinson. But the cinema ceased operation around 1921, and the premises were converted to a plating works. Later it became a shop, but was demolished in the 1970s and the present Spurs Shop – selling souvenirs and memorabilia connected to the football club – occupies the site today.

WYVERN ELECTRIC THEATRE / TOTTENHAM CINEMA

193-195, High Road, South Tottenham, N15 4NP
(corner of Ipplepen Road)

Opened 1910. Closed 1922.

79

Became blouse factory, then a shop, later demolished.
Flats are now on the site.

This was a conversion of Wyvern House Assembly Rooms which were used for a variety of community uses, including dancing lessons. The cinema is first listed in the 1910 *Bioscope Annual*, with A.R. Guide as the manager, and a capacity of 200 persons. In 1911, the American Bioscope Co took over, but in April 1913 it was reopened after a short closure as the Tottenham Cinema, owned by Alec Finegold, with 350 seats.

By 1914, the Ironbridge Electrical Co. owned the cinema and continued to do so until it closed in 1922. The building became a small factory manufacturing ladies blouses, but later became a branch of the London Co-operative Society, who expanded from their adjacent premises at 197 High Road. This stretch of the High Road was then a prosperous shopping parade.

The former Wyvern / Tottenham Cinema, after conversion to a shop, photo-graphed in 1970 shortly before the area was comprehensively redeveloped, and Ipplepen Road disappeared.

(Kevin Wheelan)

In the 1960s, the area was comprehensively re-developed, and all the shops were demolished except for a few close to South Tottenham station which still survive today. Ipplepen Road completely vanished in this scheme, and the cinema site is now covered by houses and flats.

CORNER PICTURE THEATRE / CORNER CINEMA

820, Seven Sisters Road, Tottenham, N15 5PQ
(at Seven Sisters Corner)

Opened April 1911. Closed 27th August 1960.
Became a bingo club, then a music venue/nightclub.
Later demolished – offices now on site.

Constructed on a vacant site at the busy junction of several tram routes, and close to Seven Sisters railway station, this was a project of National Theatres de Luxe Ltd. The corner entrance of the cinema was surmounted by a tall dome with some elaborate decoration. Inside, there was seating in stalls and a small balcony, and the Bioscope annual directory gives the seating capacity as 700.

The earliest advertisement, in the *Weekly Herald*, appears on April 14th 1911, but the cinema is likely to have opened before

The Corner Picture Theatre, soon after opening in 1911.
(Bruce Castle Museum (Haringey Culture, Libraries and Learning))

then. Although advertised as "The Corner Electric Theatre", the name "Corner Picture Theatre" appears on the building in early photographs. Amongst the first films on offer were *The Greater Call* starring Alice Donovan, and *Romance of Hefty Burke* with Richard Neill. More serious fare was offered for Monday April 20th – *Hamlet* ("Shakespeare's Great Masterpiece").

But the proprietors were soon in trouble for showing films on Sundays and on Good Friday. This was not allowed by the licencing authority – the Middlesex County Council – the only exception being certain charity shows which had to obtain special permission. It was not until the 1930s that regular Sunday opening was allowed – as late as 1937 in the Wood Green area- and even then, opening hours and film titles were strictly controlled, and a proportion of profits had to be distributed to local charities.

The *Weekly Herald* of May 19th 1911 reports that the Corner was prosecuted for showing films on April 2, 8, 14, 16 and 23. They were fined £2.00, plus costs, for the first offence and 10/- (50p) for the other dates.

This early setback does not seem to have harmed the cinema's fortunes, but it soon changed ownership to a company called Whitechapel Wharf Ltd. By 1914, the proprietor was Israel Hooberman, and in 1926, Ben Jay was the owner. By 1938, Davies Cinemas had taken over- they also operated the Pavilion/Florida in Tottenham High Road and advertised the two cinemas jointly – and seating capacity was given as a more comfortable 540 in a trade directory. The cinema name was by now plain "Corner".

In 1939, the architects Howes and Jackman were engaged to rebuild the Corner as a more modern cinema – the same architects had successfully transformed the Tottenham Pavilion into the Florida a year earlier. But these plans were thwarted when it was discovered that the Council planned to widen Seven Sisters Road outside the cinema. This would have meant "stepping back" the new cinema building, resulting in a loss of seating capacity which rendered the scheme unviable, so nothing happened. Then the War came and plans for both road-widening and a new cinema were forgotten.

After the War the cinema continued to operate until a

general decline in audiences, and closure came on 27th August 1960, with two far from new films: *The Flame and the Arrow* starring Burt Lancaster and Virginia Mayo, made in 1950, and *Shoot-Out at Medicine Bend* featuring Randolph Scott dating from 1957.

The Corner with its simplified exterior, operating as the Club Noreik, photo-graphed in 1970.

(Kevin Wheelan)

The building was soon converted to a bingo club, and was then purchased by Laurie Boost who named the building "Club Noreik" – Noreik being the name of Laurie's soon – Kieron – spelt backwards. Bingo continued during the week, but at weekends the old cinema became a music venue, and several performers who are now well-known names had some of their early performances here. For example, The Rolling Stones appeared on 28th December 1963 (in an "All-Night Rave"), Gene Vincent appeared on 15th August 1964, and The Who performed on 23rd January 1965.

Gradually, bingo ceased and the building became a full-time music venue and nightclub. By the 1970s, the music on offer had become more in the Reggae style, reflecting the changing nature of the area's population. Some famous names continued to appear, for example Desmond Dekker and Gregory Isaacs.

The Club closed in 1979, and the building was demolished in 1980. A small office block – Apex House – was built, occupied by Haringey Council. And Seven Sisters Road was never widened!

Jimmy Green, writing in "How Things Were" in 1982, recalled the Corner:
"It was cheaper and rougher than the Peoples Palace, we used to pay a halfpenny on Saturday mornings. They had the silent films with fleas jumping all over you at the same time. They used to have a piano going and the little balls used to jump on the song as it was being played. They had Pearl White, Eddie Polo, The Phantom and the Invisible Man. If the picture was lousy, or the piano player, we used to get hold of all the seats, they weren't attached to the floor very well, and pull them, everyone went with them- down they'd go. There was an old boy worked there who we called 'Kipper feet', years later I met him and had a chat with him about it. I said 'Do you remember when you worked at the Corner Picturehouse?' and he said 'yes, you bleeders used to drive me mad!'"

Keith Bailey, writing in a letter to Kevin Wheelan in 1984, recalled the Corner:
"My father after starting as a projectionist was manager at the Corner and later the Florida at Tottenham as well. When Western Electric Sound was installed in 1930, it was battery powered- there were two sets of batteries, one of which was in use whilst the other was being charged, it took all night. For a period of its life, the Corner was not connected to the electricity supply but used its own petrol-driven generator and a separate motor generator for the projectors. There was always a drop in screen illumination when it was time for the film reels to be changed over. The Corner had a small circle, and access to the projector box was up the main stairs, across the circle and down the back stairs halfway because the box was between circle and stalls. Originally the entrance to the building, which was literally on the corner, was surmounted by a glass dome and flag pole. When 'King Kong' was released in 1933, as a press stunt my grandfather fixed a large stuffed monkey on the dome holding onto the flagpole, however this caused such traffic chaos at the junction that they were forced to remove it by the Council."

GRAND PICTURE HOUSE / TOTTENHAM PAVILION / FLORIDA

678, High Road, Tottenham, N17 0AE

Opened 15th April 1911. Closed 15th May 1971.

Demolished. A showroom and light industrial unit were built on site, now converted to supermarket with flats above.

This cinema was built and first operated as The Grand by Robert C Buchanan, trading as Cecil Cinemas, who also owned cinemas at Crouch End (which opened on the same day) and Turnpike Lane. The building, constructed on a vacant site, had a seating capacity of 750. By 1914, the owners are shown as

The Grand, renamed as The Tottenham Pavilion, photographed in 1923. Not a political demonstration outside, but a publicity stunt for the film "Brothers Under the Skin".
(Cinema Theatre Association, Tony Moss Collection)

Adelphi Pictures Ltd, but by 1915 it was operated by Messrs A Dubowski and M. Michaels. They renamed it Tottenham Pavilion in 1920, with a reduced seating capacity of 710, but by 1926 it had changed hands again to Mr Ben Jay.

The Pavilion was rebuilt in 1938 as The Florida, and featured this fine frontage, photo-graphed soon after re-building.

(Cinema Theatre Association Archive)

The main Florida sign was later removed, as in this photo-graph taken in 1970.

(Kevin Wheelan)

The interior of
The Florida,
designed by
Mollo and Egan.

*(Cinema
Theatre
Association
Archive)*

After alterations for showing sound films, Davies Cinemas – who also operated the Corner Cinema near Seven Sisters – took over in 1935. In 1937, they engaged architects Howes and Jackman to completely rebuild the Pavilion, demolishing the whole of the building except for the left-hand wall. The new cinema, renamed The Florida, opened on January 27th 1938 after just 16 weeks of building work. The interior decoration was by the well-known design partnership of Mollo and Egan, whose work can still be seen in the interior of the Phoenix Cinema, East Finchley. At Tottenham their work was confined to grille work around the screen area, and some decorative plaques on the side walls.

The Florida had a seating capacity of 754:522 in the stalls and 232 in the circle. To provide this number of seats on the relatively small site, the foyer space was minimal.

The Florida survived the 1950s and 60s when many other local cinemas closed, but it's final show came on May 15th 1971, with a revival of two previously released comedy films: *Carry on Camping* staring Sid James, Barbara Windsor, etc together with *That Riviera Touch*, the second cinema outing for the comedians Morecambe and Wise (generally considered an unsuccessful film).

The building was demolished and replaced by the offices, showroom and factory unit of Diana Martin Ladieswear. Around 2005, that company moved out and the building was converted to a supermarket with flats above, named Diana Martin House.

Keith Bailey, writing in a letter to Kevin Wheelan in 1984, recalled the Florida:

"My mother worked as a projectionist at the Florida and my father was manager for a time. We think it was the last cinema in the area completed just before war broke out in 1939, which meant that it's magnificent exterior lighting was kept dark until regulations were relaxed, and we have a photograph entitled 'The lights go on again after 10 years- April 2nd 1949'. For its time the Florida was very modern, all electric apart from gas secondary lighting. There was a large lighting switchboard in the operating box to control auditorium and stage lighting and the two sets of stage curtains. Ventilation was by a large mechanical plant on the roof which washed, heated, scented and distributed air to various parts of the building.

There was always a queue at the Florida from 6.15 until the start of the last film, and often the canopy over the entrance was used to stage promotions using 'monsters' for one film and massive shields to promote 'Henry V' when shown. The vestibule though wide was quite small and the paybox tiny, with just about room for the cashier provided she was not too large!"

Carol Davis, who now lives in South Wales, recalls:

"I was born in Argyle Road and the Florida was about a two minute walk away from home. The first film I recall seeing was 'Alice in Wonderland' which my older sister Hazel took me to when I was only 4 years old. She went off with some friends and left me on my own for most of the film and I was terrified, especially when Alice grew larger! There were also Saturday morning pictures and I remember some films in 3D (specs provided). I often went to see films there with my parents on a weekday evening as they went regularly every week. I remember the lovely woman who sat in a tiny cubicle taking the money and giving us our tickets- she was plump and had Marcel-waved dyed blonde hair and very red lipstick. My parents called her by her first name but I don't remember what it was.

Among the films I remember were 'Loving You' (my first sight of Elvis Presley) and 'The Pride and the Passion' (Sophia Loren). In the scene where huge flaming balls of hay are rolled down a hill into the enemy army, a wit at the back of the cinema called out" great balls of fire!" much to the amusement of everyone. The Florida was a small cinema with an intimate atmosphere – such a shame that it was allowed to get run down and then demolished."

IMPERIAL ELECTRIC THEATRE / IMPERIAL / ESSOLDO

290-294 West Green Road, Tottenham, N15 3QR

Opened 6th November 1913. Closed 31st May 1958.
Became a warehouse, then a carpet shop, now place of worship.

This cinema was constructed on a vacant site by the West Green Electric Theatre Company and designed by architect E.A.Thorne. He produced an attractive frontage with three round windows and decorative plasterwork in the form of bunches of grapes. Inside, there was minimal decoration, but columns on the side walls were topped by plaster cherubs and more bunches of grapes. Beyond the small foyer, there were seats for around 550 patrons on a single floor. The opening films included *The Two Divers*, produced in Italy, and *The Only Chance*, an American production starring Tom Mix. A *Pathe Gazette* newsreel was also shown.

The cinema was acquired by Charles Wright in 1916 and redecorated throughout- seating capacity in the Kinematograph Year Book was then given as 600. By 1917 the Lion Cinematograph Co. had taken over.

The cinema was adapted for sound films by 1931 when it was owned by Haman Sado. The seating capacity was now a more comfortable 472. He sold it to Harold Brown in 1942, who at first traded as the Trafalgar Film Corporation, but later as Mayfair Circuit (Tottenham) Ltd. In October 1943, Harold Brown informed the licencing authority – the Middlesex County Council-that the cinema had been acquired by the large national ABC chain – a surprising move as this major circuit did not often acquire small properties, and there was already an ABC-owned Ritz cinema nearby at Turnpike Lane, opened in 1935. However, the deal was not concluded and Mayfair remained in control until 24th August 1945, when the large national chain of Essoldo acquired the cinema. They renamed the cinema Essoldo, and made some improvements, including fitting a larger screen to accommodate "Cinemascope" films in the 1950s. But the general decline in cinema-going had begun, and the cinema closed on 31st May 1958. The closing films were *Witness for the Prosecution* starring Tyrone Power and Marlene Dietrich, and *The Betrayal* featuring Philip Friend.

The building became a warehouse for the Atlas Lighting Co, but by the 1960s had become a discount carpet shop- ends of rolls, etc – which it was to remain for the next 40 years. Inside, the screen was removed but the projection box and the plaster cherubs could still be seen. The carpet store closed in 2000, and after a period lying empty, the building is now used as a place of worship, with the Imperial name once again on the frontage. The plaster grapes have been nicely restored, but inside a false ceiling has been erected hiding the original ceiling, although traces of the cherubs and fruit can still be seen.

The exterior of the Imperial as it appears today, in religious use.

(Peter Staveley)

BRUCE GROVE CINEMA

118, Bruce Grove, Tottenham, N17 6UR

Opened 14th July 1921. Closed 31st August 1963.
Became a bingo club, currently divided between snooker (lower
part) and place of worship (upper part)

In January 1920, a prospectus was issued by the Tottenham Cinema & Entertainment Company, for shares of £1 each, to raise funds to build a cinema seating 2500, plus a ballroom, on vacant land adjacent to the railway in Bruce Grove. The shares issue was successful, and local architect Charles E. Blackbourn was engaged to design the building which opened as the Bruce Grove Super Cinema in July 1921. The ballroom adjoining the cinema, with its own entrance further north along Bruce Grove, was not completed until 1923.

The new cinema was a most impressive building, far larger than any existing cinema in the local area, with a tall tower feature, surmounted by columns and a cupola, at the entrance nearest to Bruce Grove station. At night, this was illuminated by

Bruce Grove in 1928, with the Bruce Grove Cinema to the right.
(Bruce Castle Museum (Haringey Culture, Libraries and Learning))

91

numerous bulbs. Inside, seating was arranged in stalls and balcony for 1,791 people – slightly less than the original plans. Advertising in the *Weekly Herald* stated it was "the cheeriest and most imposing cinema in the district" and that it was "not a makeshift building. It was constructed especially for a cinema...". This may be a jibe at the nearby Canadian Rink cinema, which was converted from a roller-skating rink.

The opening films were *The Mark of Zorro* starring Douglas Fairbanks and *Cupid Hires a Taxi Cab* with Ray Berger. At first, the silent films were accompanied by piano and orchestra, but in 1926, an organ was installed. This was no doubt a reaction to the fact that the nearby Palace Cinema in the High Road had installed a Wurlitzer organ in 1925. At Bruce Grove, the new organ was British-made by Jardine with 3 manuals (keyboards) and 26 ranks (sets) of pipes installed in two chambers either side of the screen. It was really more of a "straight" church-like organ than a cinema organ and the opening organist was Herbert Griffiths.

Equipment for sound films – a "British Talking Picture Reproducer" – was fitted around 1930 and then full rewiring followed, but in 1933 the directors decided to go for a more full-scale modernisation. The cinema closed for this work on June 23rd 1933 and reopened on August 18th 1933. Ideal Kinema magazine reported that "the work was carried out in a little over five weeks to the designs of Mr Robert Cromie, F.R.I.B.A. The interior has been gutted and the circle reconstructed. A former café/lounge at the rear of the circle has been removed and a new area of seating installed. There is a new proscenium arch with a modern rectangular opening in place of the previous rounded one". The interior also received a revised decorative scheme in a more "art-deco" fashion. The new seating must have been more spacious, because total capacity of the cinema was slightly reduced to 1,789.

Robert Cromie (1887-1971) was a prominent cinema and theatre architect, and amongst his works were the Prince of Wales theatre in London's West End and the 3,487 seat Gaumont Palace at Hammersmith, one of the largest cinemas in the London area, which is today known as the Apollo rock venue.

The organ survived this rebuild, but had fallen into disuse

and was removed in 1935. It was re-installed in the nearby High Cross Congregational Church by the firm of Gray and Davidson and re-opened there in 1937. It lasted until 1963 when most of the pipes were removed because they needed expensive repairs. Some

(Above) The Bruce Grove Cinema shortly after it was converted to a Bingo Club in 1963.

(Left) The interior of the Bruce Grove Cinema after conversion to a Bingo Club. *(Cinema Theatre Association. Tony Moss Collection)*

facing pipes were re-gilded and remained until the church was demolished in the 1980s- the present church (now known as High Cross United Reform Church) occupies the former church hall.

The cinema was acquired by Star Cinemas in 1962, but it soon fell victim to the general decline of cinema-going at that time, and closed the following year, on 31st August 1963. The final films were *Tamahine* with Nancy Kwan and Dennis Price, and *To Have and To Hold* with Ray Barrett, which was later transmitted as an episode of the TV series Edgar Wallace Mysteries.

The cinema was converted into a Star Bingo Club which it remained for many years. At some time, the top of the tower feature was removed to leave the stumpy feature which can still be seen today, and the interior was divided into two by constructing a floor from the front of the balcony to the stage area. The upper part remained on bingo, whilst the former stalls became a snooker hall. Bingo ceased in 1983, and the upper area remained empty until 1986 when it took on a bizarre role as an indoor cricket stadium (used for teaching cricket). This didn't last, and was replaced by another fad, a Qasar lazer-shooting range. After this failed, the area remained empty until the 1990s when Freedom's Ark Worship centre moved into the space. The lower part remains as The Edge snooker hall.

The adjoining ballroom remained as a dance venue until 1974, when in a surprise move, Star converted it to a 4-screen cinema thus restoring films to Bruce Grove after an 11-year interval. (See information under Studios 5,6,7,8).

Jim Clark, writing in the CTA Bulletin in 1994, recalls:
"My favourite cinema was the Bruce Grove, purpose-built in 1921 for the exhibition of silent films. Situated rather close to the railway, trains could be heard puffing their way out of Bruce Grove Station towards White Hart Lane, not very frequently but it marred the illusion of reality. With the advent of sound films, this became less noticeable and only intruded during quiet scenes.

My first memory of cinema-going at the Bruce Grove was as a "babe- in- arms" – well perhaps just outgrowing that stage but I did sit on my father's lap. Although 'The Jazz Singer' (the first sound film) must have been doing the rounds about that time, all other motion pictures were silent. I can remember seeing on the screen grown-up people moving jerkily and mouthing words for a few moments then the screen filled with print for a long time and which I was too young to read, followed by many similar sequences. Absolutely meaningless to me and very boring. The audience, including my parents, seemed much absorbed in the proceedings which to me were nothing more than a new experience.

As the family began to grow up regular visits to the "pictures" sometimes twice a week became our most prized treat, and we soon came to recognise the stars of the times – Ronald Coleman, Wallace Beery, Basil Rathbone, William Powell, etc not forgetting Mickey Mouse. All the women looked the same to me.

The main entrance to the Bruce Grove had a glamour all of its own. Up a few steps and through glass panelled doors with large curved brass handles to the centrally placed glass surrounded ticket kiosk- sometimes we took circle seats and went up the stairs which were carpeted in red rubber. The walls were studded with framed photographs of famous stars. An usherette with a torch showed us to our seats and a little man wandered up and down the aisles selling "Ices, Chocolates, Cigarettes" from a dimly lighted tray. There was a second entrance at the other end of the building for the cheap seats, 6d or 9d, and if you came in there you walked in alongside the screen and had to sit disturbingly close to it. The pictures looked long and distorted especially if you sat to the side.

It was a continuous programme, and we stayed until "this is where we came in". There would be an interval when advertisements were shown for local businesses, also trailers for next week's attractions. The 10-minute newsreel made up the complete programme lasting around 3 hours. Unless an epic film like 'Gone With The Wind' was being shown, the programme was changed twice a week plus on Sundays a couple of old films were put on which had been shown before.

It was a comfortable cinema and the fine quality screen had rounded corners and the sound system was excellent. To the bottom corner was a clock illuminated in subdued deep red for those who needed to know the time. Other cinemas never seemed so homely- I believe it was privately owned and not linked to any of the main circuits."

TOTTENHAM PALACE

421-427 High Road, Tottenham N17 6QN

Opened (for full-time films) 21st November 1924.
Closed 28th June 1969.
Became a Mecca bingo club (later Jasmine), then a place of
worship. Listed Grade II

The Palace opened on 31st August 1908 as a variety theatre, a variant of the music-hall, though offering similar entertainment. The architects were Wylson and Long who had already designed theatres at Kilburn, Walthamstow and East Ham among many others. These have all been demolished, making the Palace a rare survivor of their work. The theatre's interior was elaborately decorated, mainly in a Grecian style, with seats for around 2000 patrons in stalls, balcony and upper balcony levels.

From the start, moving pictures – the latest craze – were featured amongst the live acts on the bill. "Ruffell's Imperial Bioscope depicting all the latest events" was advertised, and the theatre had a special "biograph chamber", for the film projector, constructed at balcony level. This was quite far-sighted of the owners, as the Cinematograph Act, which would make such special rooms essential, was not enacted until almost two years later.

The proprietors were United Varieties Syndicate Ltd who successfully operated the theatre throughout the First World War, but come the 1920s they faced strong competition from the many local cinemas which had been established nearby – the large Bruce Grove Cinema opened in 1921, and right next door to the Palace, the Canadian Rink had successfully operated since 1911. Films at the Palace gradually increased in place of variety acts, especially in afternoon performances from 1922 onwards.

In 1924, the Palace and the Canadian Rink came under the same ownership, and full-time films transferred from the Canadian to the Palace. To try and retain the loyalty of the Canadian Rink patrons, the Palace was temporarily renamed

"The Canadian Cinema (Tottenham Palace)" from 21st November 1924. The opening film was *The Lady* featuring Norma Talmadge, but there were still some variety acts between the films. The former Canadian Rink cinema was converted to Tottenham Palais de Dance.

The Palace as a cinema, photographed around 1949. The name does not seem to appear on the building, the board over the door has the letters "GB" for Gaumont-British. In later years, the stonework at the top of the building was simplified and a large "PALACE" name erected in neon letters. *(Odeon Cavalcade)*

In 1925, a large chain, Provincial Cinematograph Theatres (PCT) acquired the Palace (and the Palais de Dance), and instituted improvements to the building to make it a more modern cinema. These included reducing the seating capacity to 1,379, and relocating the projection room from the conventional position at the back of the theatre, to an unusual position behind the screen on the disused variety stage, a system known as "rear-projection".

The film is projected onto the rear of the screen rather than onto the front as is normal. This system has always been rare in the UK, and is believed to operate today in only one cinema, The Kinema-in-the-Woods at Woodhall Spa, Lincolnshire. At that cinema, the film is projected onto a mirror which reflects the picture in reverse onto the back of the screen, to be viewed by the public as normal.

At Tottenham, mirrors were not used, but the film was shown back-to-front onto the rear of the screen and thus viewed the right way by the cinema patrons.

It is believed this rear-projection method was adopted because of limited space in the balcony or upper balcony to construct a projection room of adequate dimensions. Although the Palace had possessed a projection room since 1908, this was likely to have been small and not capable of being used to show films continuously. There was also plenty of room on the deep stage.

The other improvement PCT made was to install a Wurlitzer theatre organ, specially imported from the USA – only the second to be shipped over (the first had been installed at Walsall earlier in 1925). The 2-manual "Model F", organ console was installed in the orchestra pit, and the 6 ranks of pipework were installed in a specially-constructed chamber located in one of the theatre's boxes. The organ debut was on April 6th 1925 with Jack Courtnay being the opening organist.

In August 1926, the name "Palace" was restored to the building and "Canadian Cinema" was dropped.

In February 1929, PCT were acquired by the expanding Gaumont-British chain, who modified the cinema for sound films shortly afterwards. This meant the Wurlitzer organ became used less frequently, but it survived in the theatre until August 1957, when it was sold for £450 to Rye Grammar School, East Sussex. It was installed in the school hall, with the pipework at the rear of the hall's balcony, and the console at the front of the balcony. The organ is still there today- having spent longer at Rye than at the Palace – and has recently been improved and refurbished with the console being relocated to the hall's stage on a rise-and-fall lift. Regular concerts are held at the school, which is now known as Rye College.

The Palace continued under Gaumont control, which later became part of the Rank Organisation. The theatre never changed its name to Gaumont as did many other GB theatres, but a sign saying "A Gaumont Theatre" was installed over the

entrance doors and can still be seen to this day, much faded..
The general decline in cinema attendances caught up with
the Palace in 1969 and it closed on June 28th with the films *File
of the Golden Goose* with Yul Brynner and Edward Woodward,
together with *Sam Whiskey* starring Burt Reynolds.

(Left) The Palace in 1964, with simplified roofline and "Palace" name. Notice the former original Canadian Rink cinema to the left, converted to a shop. *(Cinema Theatre Association Archive)*

(Below) The interior of The Palace, when in use as Bingo club, photographed in 1993. *(Jeffrey Mackenzie)*

The building became a Mecca bingo club which operated successfully for many years, and was later operated by Jasmine. They moved the operation to a new building at Tottenham Hale Retail Park in February 1996 (this has since closed), and after a short period of disuse, the Palace became a place of worship known as the Palace Cathedral, which it still is today. The building was listed at Grade II in December 1992.

The building's ornate interior is generally intact and in good condition with the upper balcony being of particular interest as it has been disused for many years, the bingo operation not using that area, and it probably saw little use in its latter cinema days. It still retains some very old seating, possibly dating from the theatre's opening in 1908.

John Leach, a former cinema projectionist, recalls:
"When I was at projectionist training school in 1963, one of the fellow students worked at the Palace Tottenham, so the teachers always had to remember to point out that the film lace-up was reversed for that cinema (rear projection). I was told they had a specially adapted "Kalee" projector with the sound head on the opposite side. The student told me that sometimes a person would mistakenly walk across the stage whilst the film was being shown so the audience got a large shadow outline of them on the screen!"

Jim Clark, writing in the *CTA Bulletin* in 1994, recalls:
"The Tottenham Palace was an Edwardian music hall that was converted for showing films in an unusual way. As it had a large backstage area, the projection was from behind the screen and therefore had to be shown back to front so that the audience saw it the right way round. Later on, when the screen deteriorated and developed some small holes, from certain positions you might get the bright light of the projector dazzling your eyes. On a Friday night there would often be a few paltry music hall turns in addition to the films. Very poor stuff I thought, perhaps having just seen an exciting gangster film."

STUDIOS 5, 6, 7, 8

113 Bruce Grove, Tottenham N17 6UR

Opened 14th July 1974. Closed 12th December 1981.

Became a banqueting suite

This building was originally the Bruce Grove Ballroom, opened in 1923 by the same company who operated the adjacent Bruce Grove Cinema, and designed by the same architect, Charles E. Blackbourn. The ballroom was located on the first floor, with shops at ground floor level, and there was a car park at the rear. The cinema closed in 1963, but the ballroom continued. In 1974, the Star Group, who had acquired the cinema and had operated it as a bingo club, decided to convert the ballroom into a 4-secreen "studio cinema" restoring films to the Tottenham area which had been without a cinema since the Florida closed in 1971.

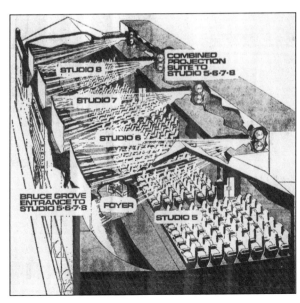

The layout of the Studio Cinemas, from the *Tottenham Weekly Herald* of July 1974.

(Bruce Castle Museum (Haringey Culture, Libraries and Learning))

It was divided into 4 small cinemas, seating 107,110, 115 and 118, and a new projection unit was built on steel stilts at the rear of the building. This was equipped with the facility for the projectors to be linked so that the same film could be shown in all of the four studios almost simultaneously, if desired. The designers of the new cinema were Jack Cornelius Ltd together with Star Group's own personnel.

Exterior of Studios 5,6,7,8 in 1975.
(Cinema Theatre Association Archive)

The *Weekly Herald* said "the new Studios typify the trend in cinema development throughout the country. The four intimate auditoria will offer cinemagoers comfort coupled with a wider choice of programme...the décor is in Vymura, Formica and velvet-look flocked wall finishes with thick purple wall-to-wall carpeting. There are comfortable wedge-back seats and streamlined screens". The new cinema was named Studios 5,6,7 and 8, because the Star Group already operated a 4–screen cinema in London's West End – named Scene 1,2,3 and 4 – and numbered the Tottenham cinemas to follow on from these four.

The opening films were selected to cater mainly for an adult audience, ranging from *Dillinger* starring Warren Oates and Richard Dreyfuss, to a revival of the 1961 epic *The Guns of Navarone* with Gregory Peck and David Niven, also a Kung–Fu film with Bruce Lee and Bonnie & Clyde, made in 1967. Studio 8 specialised in "continental films" – the opening title being *Love Making-Hot Style!*

The new cinema seemed reasonably successful at first, continuing to specialise mainly in action and crime movies, and lasted until closure on 12th December 1981, probably killed off by the rise in home video and the failure to attract up-to-date big releases. The closing films were *Stir Crazy*, *Blood Beach* and *Zombie Flesh Eaters* (a double bill) and *Force Five*, with *Teenage Fever* and *Deep Thought* as the "continental" films in Studio 8!

The building remained empty and derelict for a couple of years, but around 1984 it had its internal divisions removed and was restored to be one large space and became a banqueting and function suite called the Regency.

Film were also shown at:

MUNICIPAL BATHS HALL

Town Hall Approach, Tottenham, N15 4RX

The Walturdaw Company presented films in this hall, adjacent to Tottenham Town Hall and the Swimming Baths, just for a short period from October 1909 to early 1910. The shows were on Saturdays and Mondays. Walturdaw already operated the nearby People's Palace in Forster Road as a full-time cinema. The Municipal Baths Hall was unlikely to have met the requirements of the Cinematograph Act 1910, which is probably the reason for its rapid demise as a cinema. The site is now occupied by the Bernie Grant Theatre, so a tradition of performance continues.

Wood Green

ELECTROSCOPE / PALAIS DE LUXE / REX

18, Station Road, Wood Green, N22 6UW

Opened 18th December 1909. Closed 2nd May 1964.
Became a bingo club, then demolished. Now a vacant site, used
as a car park, with mini-cab office on site of entrance foyer.

This cinema started life as part of a building which also included a roller-skating rink, and the entrance was at first in River Park Road. It was operated by a company called North London Skating Rink Ltd and Electroscope Theatre, and had around 400 seats. The adjoining skating rink was meant to open at the same time, but it was not ready and opened later, on January 29th 1910, as the North London Rink.

Opening publicity at Wood Green invited skaters to "drop in at the Electroscope Theatre adjoining the rink and spend time in comfort and pleasure. Teas gratis at 4.30 p.m." The Metropolitan Tramways Band entertained at the opening- the tram depot was on the other side of River Park Road, a site now in use as a bus garage.

The craze for roller-skating proved not to last, and both rink and cinema appear to have closed within a year or so after opening. But in 1913, the cinema part of the building expanded into the rink area of the building, and was able to gain a more prominent entrance on the busier Station Road, in former shop premises, linked to the auditorium behind by a passage. An elaborate, if narrow, frontage was erected, and it was renamed Palais de Luxe.

It re-opened on 8th November 1913, advertising itself as "the finest and most up-to-date picture house in the district". The Weekly Herald stated that it now had 986 seats, but a more likely

The Palais de Luxe pictured in 1938, closed for rebuilding into The Rex. *(Cinema Theatre Association Archive / Tony Moss Collection)*

figure is 850, on one level, and it was now owned by Palais de Luxe Ltd. By 1928 the owners were River Park Cinemas, who also owned the Premier at Harringay, and in September 1930 they adapted the cinema to show sound films – "talkies". But in January 1938 the two cinemas were sold to Harry Pearl who traded as Gaywood Cinemas, and seating capacity at that time was 694.

The Palais had, since 1934, faced stiff competition from the newer and grander Gaumont Palace nearby, so Gaywood decided to modernise the Palais to become more competitive. It closed on 22nd January 1938, and posters outside advised patrons that the cinema was "Closed for Extensive Reconstruction into North London's Finest Miniature Super". Re-opening was set for 9th March 1938, but in the event was delayed until 14th March when it re-opened, as The Rex, with the appropriately named film *Back in Circulation* starring Joan Blondell. Seating capacity was now 696. An artist's impression in the *Weekly Herald* shows an attractive art-deco frontage with a curved design with ribbed plasterwork and the name "Rex" in deco-style letters on a free-standing sign. But the earliest pictures we have, from the 1960s,

The rebuilt Palais De Luxe, as The Rex, pictured in 1960. *(Cinema Theatre Association Archive / Mike Thomas)*

show a much plainer, flat frontage, although with the same attractive lettering. Correspondence in the Middlesex County Council archives suggests that this modernisation was the work of architect F. E. Bromige, who had also designed the alterations to Gaywood's other cinema at Harringay.

In the 1950s the Rex was acquired by Southan Morris (S.M. Associated Cinemas Ltd) but in August 1954, the larger Essoldo circuit took over. They often renamed their properties with the circuit name, but at Wood Green the Rex name survived.

This author remembers the Rex as a rather run-down and shabby place, and rarely went there. He can remember being taken as a child by his exasperated mother one wet afternoon during the school holidays, when she had run out of things to keep him amused, and we had already seen the films at the other cinemas. We saw a revival of *The Big Country*, made in 1958 and starring Gregory Peck, which seemed to me to be an interminably long and boring Western. Whenever it appears on television nowadays, I am reminded of that wet afternoon at the Rex!

The general decline in attendances caught up with the Rex and it closed on May 2nd 1964 with the films *The Red Beret* starring Alan Ladd and *The Man from Laramie* with James Stewart. It became a bingo club which lasted until 1977 when it was demolished, along with all the adjoining shops on that side of Station Road, for an office development for Haringey Council. The site of the auditorium was not actually built on, and serves today as a small open car park for the staff at Alexandra House, whilst a temporary building, which is used as a minicab office, sits on the space once occupied by the entrance foyer.

Matthew Oliver, who now lives in Christchurch, Dorset, recalls:
"In 1945, at the age of 13, I lived at 17 Pelham Road, Wood Green, and my gran lived at No 15. But on Shrove Tuesday, at about 5.00p.m., a V2 rocket hit the back of No 15 at the time my Gran was in the garden, she was never ever found. As for me I was in the Rex Cinema in Station Road, thanks to Gran who gave me 1/- (5p) at dinner time, otherwise I would have been in the house. Later that year I was 14 years old and left school and my first job was at the Rex as a trainee projectionist. I later worked at the Odeon Southgate, then the Odeon Muswell Hill, and after National Service back to Muswell Hill before going to the Empire, Leicester Square until 1958. After some time in other jobs, I retired in 1989 and moved to Christchurch and within weeks became a volunteer projectionist at the Regent Centre. So you can see from the age of 14 projection was in my blood!

David McGillivray, film director and writer, who now lives in Islington recalls:
"I grew up in Palmers Green and went most weeks to the Odeon and Rex Wood Green and Regal Harringay. By the time I was 12, my peer group was managing to bluff its way into "X" films, off limits in those days to the under-16s. It sounded easy- "I know you're not sixteen, but I'm letting you in because we need the money" the cashier at the Rex Wood Green told my friend Derek Gray. But I was too lily-livered to join these escapades. I thought I would be frightened to death, a possibility which, according to the posters ("£10,000 if you die of fright") was all too likely.

When I turned 14 I felt that the time had come to face the challenge, and my mother took me to the ABC Turnpike Lane to see 'Gorgo' in which a dinosaur trampled London. She thought it was ridiculous and I realised for the first time that most horror films are like Christmas- anticipating it is better than experiencing it. I think this is what Karl Boehm meant in 'Peeping Tom' when he said "The most frightening thing in the world is fear itself". Much later, I made horror films."

LORDSHIP LANE CINEMATOGRAPH THEATRE

4 Lordship Lane, Wood Green, N22 6EJ
(Due to renumbering, present-day address would be 737-9
Lordship Lane)

Opened 31st December 1909. Closed 1920
Became a furniture repository, later bingo club and dance studio.
Later demolished, part of Hollywood Green development on site.

A development of a local company, Wood Green Market & Cinematograph Theatre Ltd, the building was designed by George Duckworth and built on part of Alsford's timber yard. The cinema was on the first floor, and on the ground floor was a market hall.

The opening night on New Year's Eve 1909 was described as a "dress rehearsal and private view" and the public shows commenced on January 1st 1910. The local press reported that

The Lordship Lane Cinematograph Theatre pictured in 1913.

(Bruce Castle Museum (Haringey Culture, Libraries and Learning))

there were around 560 seats, that the screen was 20ft by 15ft. and that there were continuous shows from 3-11, Saturdays at 2, "pictures only but with Allefex and Vivophone machines installed" – these provided sound effects to the silent films. There were also "orchestral effects" and "speaking pictures" where an "effects man" explained the action of the film with dialogue – he was often located behind the screen. The *Bioscope* magazine rather demeaned this practice, saying "it was only practiced in the cheaper houses".

The Lordship Lane had particularly dramatic advertising, probably initiated by the enthusiastic manager, Tom Mercer, who always seemed to ensure the cinema was mentioned in the local press each week. Films of recent local events were often shown, for example a swimming gala in Broomfield Park, Palmers Green, in July 1910 and a sports day at Wood Green.

In 1913, the cinema started to open on Sundays, provoking much controversy in the local press, and indeed Sunday opening continued to be a thorny problem for local cinemas for many years. The licencing authority, Middlesex County Council, did not allow it and some cinemas, such as the Corner at Tottenham, were prosecuted. Some of the proceeds from Sunday openings generally had to be donated to local charities, and it was not until the 1930s that Sunday opening was universally allowed in the Borough.

Also in 1913, the Lordship Lane started to suffer from stiff local competition when three other cinemas opened in Wood Green, all larger and more well-appointed. Tom Mercer also left the same year under something of a cloud, and was later prosecuted for theft of National Insurance cards and stamps.

During 1914 and 1915, the cinema was sometimes advertised as "The Market Cinema". It seems to have closed around 1920 although there is no definite date in the local press.

A 1921 street directory shows the building as occupied by Garner's Furniture Depository. Much later, from the 1950s, the upper floor was occupied by the Harry Boult School of Dancing, and from the 1960s this part was also used for bingo in the evenings- Wood Green's first bingo club. The ground floor continued to be used for storage and as a garage for removals vans and coaches.

In the Haringey Central Area Plans of 1976, the building was due to be demolished for a revised road layout and an office development. It was temporarily used as an indoor market (reverting to its 1910 origins) before demolition in 1999, but rather than offices, a leisure development of bars, restaurants and a 6-screen cinema – Hollywood Green – was erected on the site. So today's patrons of the Vue Cinema are watching films on the same site as the Cinematograph back in 1909.

WOOD GREEN ELECTRIC PALACE / CROWN PICTURE PALACE

16 High Road, Wood Green, N22 6BX
(NE corner of Whymark Avenue)

Opened 1910. Closed 1920. Became a shop, later demolished, Unity College and a shop on site.

This small cinema first appears in a 1910/11 street directory, and was converted from a piano shop which had been built over the front garden of a Victorian villa. The Bioscope Annual for 1911 shows the proprietors as Electric Coliseums Ltd. In September 1911, the cinema was renamed Crown and taken over by Moss Cohen. The seating capacity then was 175.

Such a small cinema would find it hard to compete with the larger and grander cinemas built in Wood Green – there were 3 opened in 1913 alone- and it seems to have closed by 1920. It reverted to being a shop, occupied at first by a confectioners, later a piano shop again, Parker's.

Much later, in the 1970s, the building was demolished along with the adjoining two shops and replaced by a new building currently used as Unity College. The ground floor remains in retail use, at present a fashion shop. Some idea of the appearance of the original building can be gained by looking at No 14 High Road on the opposite corner, which is one of the last remaining Victorian houses with a shop built in front, although much rebuilt.

Ajello's Piano Shop in Wood Green High Road, on the corner of Whymark Avenue, which was converted into the Wood Green Electric Cinema in 1910.
(Bruce Castle Museum (Haringey Culture, Libraries and Learning))

CENTRAL / NEW CENTRAL

35 Station Road, Wood Green, N22 6UX
(East corner of Brabant Road)

Opened 23rd October 1913. Closed 1933.
Became a boxing/wrestling ring, then a warehouse. Later demolished, apartments and a showroom on site.

Built on an empty site by owner Mr N.H.Tranah, it was opened by the Chair of Wood Green Council, Thomas Muskett, J.P. The *Sentinel* newspaper reported that there was seating for 860 on one level and that "the first audience heard Mr H Bryant and Miss Doris Smerdon sing in fine style. But although you do not get those things at the ordinary performance you do get the accompaniment of the Cinephonium, the wonderful instrument that is equal to an orchestra and is controlled by Mr Allen the clever pianist. Added to *Hewson's News Pictures* and the best of films are free tea and biscuits between 2.30 and 5.30".

Despite the opening of the Palais de Luxe Cinema almost opposite in November 1913, the Central seems to have been a success. By 1921, ownership had changed to Parkault Ltd, and then in 1924, Attractive Cinemas (Wood Green) Ltd, under the directorship of Ralph Specterman, had taken over.

A surviving programme from 1928 features films such as *Moulin Rouge* starring Olga Tschechowa and *Tenderloin* with Dolores Costello. The programme continues: "Afternoons out at the Pictures are the happiest times of the week – It's such a comfort to know – before you go – that a good time's ahead. The name CENTRAL fixes all that! The healthy excitement of first-class entertainment in a quiet cosy theatre is a happy programme for any afternoon- there's only one price for the afternoon show- it's 6d". Films were accompanied by "our NEW orchestra of skilled musicians".

Two years later the cinema frontage was simplified, and the interior was re-seated and re-decorated, with equipment for showing sound films installed, re-opening as the New Central on June 16th 1930. The opening film was *Sunny Side Up* featuring Janet Gaynor. At first a mix of "talkies" and silent films were shown.

But a sign of troubled times ahead appeared in a newspaper report in February 1933. The owners of the New Central – by then Wood Green Cinemas Ltd – were prosecuted for showing films to under-age children in November 1932. Their counsel said that "it was one of the smallest cinemas in the district and could not compete with big combines who had first pick of the films for renting and left only residue".

The New Central closed in 1933 – the last local advertisement appearing in May. No doubt the start of building for the vast Gaumont Palace cinema around the corner hastened the end (The Gaumont opened in March 1934).

The building became the Central Ring, used for boxing and wrestling matches, first advertising in January 1934. Later it became a warehouse used by Cakebread Robey, the well-known local builder's merchants.

The former Central Cinema in use as a warehouse, photographed shortly before demolition in 1970. *(Kevin Wheelan)*

In the Haringey Central Area Plans, the building was due to be demolished to provide space for a road interchange connected with a new relief road, and for an office building. Demolition followed around 1973 and an office block was erected, used by Haringey Council, with the frontage specially curved to fit round the new road interchange. The relief road scheme was later dropped, and Brabant Road continued undisturbed.

Then in 2003, this building was demolished and replaced by Eclipse House, an apartment block with a retail showroom on the ground floor. This building also has a curved front, just in case the relief road still appears.

PICTURE PALLADIUM / PALLADIUM

46 High Road, Wood Green, N22 6BX

Opened October 1913. Closed 29th November 1937.
Demolished for an extension to Marks & Spencer store.

This cinema was built on the site of a Victorian house, which had been in use as a doctor's surgery, by Wood Green Picture Palladium Ltd. Although it was the largest cinema to be built in the area to date- with 1,500 seats in stalls and balcony - the opening seems to have attracted little publicity locally and the exact date cannot be discovered.

The Kinematograph Weekly of 13th November 1913 reports that the Picture Palladium "had opened last month. When lighted up after dusk from the great shell portico to the roof with thousands of electric bulbs, its noble façade becomes the

(Above) The Picture Palladium photographed shortly after opening in 1913. *(Cinema Theatre Association archive / Tony Moss Collection)*

(Right) Cover of a programme from the Picture Palladium from December 1913. *(Cinema Museum London)*

cynosure of all eyes a long distance away".

A surviving programme from December 1913 shows the films *The Girl and the Greaser* and *The Sleeping Beauty*, with a *Pathe Gazette* newsreel – and "Clarendon Speaking Pictures – a selection from our repertoire". This was an early attempt at synchronised sound films, using a gramophone and other effects machines. The manager is shown as Dudley Wynton, and the programme cover has the reassuring notice that "This building is disinfected throughout with Jeyes Fluid"! The cinema was equipped with a pipe organ, make unknown.

In the early hours of April 9th 1915, the cinema was badly damaged by a fire, believed to have been caused by a lighted cigarette end. The *Weekly Herald*, in reporting the fire, finally gives us a description of the interior when it opened: "The vestibules, bedecked with floral devices and richly carpeted, led into a well-upholstered hall which was capable of seating upwards of 1500. Unlike the average picture hall it boasted an orchestra and was also fitted with an organ. On each of the side walls were large pictures which, with transparent electric lighting were always a source of admiration. Each side of the screen was a handsome pillar. The auditorium consisted of a ground floor and balcony which ran across the rear end of the hall only".

The Picture Palladium with simplified frontage and shortened name, probably done after the fire of 1915.

(Cinema Theatre Association archive / Tony Moss Collection)

The front of the building was unaffected by the fire. The damage was estimated to be in the region of £10,000 to £15,000, but luckily it was insured and rebuilding was fairly rapid, the cinema re-opening on 6th September 1915. The *Weekly Herald* reported that the rebuilt cinema "has had more money spent on it than was laid out on the original building. More comfortable than before, with seating for same number, larger screen, more powerful organ, more attractive vestibule and with a ladies orchestra of six instruments". The main film on the re-opening night was *Five Nights* a British production in 5 reels from the novel by Victoria Cross. The *Herald* usefully informed us that "the film was recently banned by the Chief Constable of Preston, but the authorities here are evidently not of the same frame of mind"! At some stage, the name was shortened to just Palladium, and the cinema was equipped for sound films from April 7th 1930, when seating capacity was reduced slightly to 1184.

In 1937, the adjacent Marks and Spencer store wished to expand and acquired the Palladium Cinema. The *Weekly Herald* announced that the cinema "would be closed from November 29th to be demolished for a department store", but as this was a Monday it is more likely the last films were shown on the preceding Sunday or Saturday. On the Saturday night, the films were *The Thirteenth Chair* with May Whitty and Lewis Stone and *A Penny Pool* starring Tommy Fields.

An auction of the contents was held at the cinema on November 30th, and the building was demolished soon afterwards. The new Marks and Spencer store was constructed, and still occupies the site today.

GAUMONT PALACE / GAUMONT / ODEON

9 The Broadway, High Road, Wood Green, N22 6DS

Opened 26th March 1934. Closed 7th January 1984.
Became a bingo hall, with banqueting suite in former café area.
Now a religious meeting hall – Dominion Centre – and nightclub in café area. Listed Grade II*

This was the largest and most luxurious cinema to be built in the Borough. It was built on the site of Gladstone Gardens, a public garden which had been formed from the grounds of The Elms, a large house which had been demolished. When Wood Green Council developed other public open-space at White Hart Lane playing fields, it decided to sell off the gardens for re-development. As early as 1906, the site was earmarked for a music hall, but nothing happened until 1933 when a row of shops with flats above was built, with a space behind for a large cinema, the bulk of the auditorium therefore being cleverly concealed from the street. It was first planned that the new cinema would be an Astoria Theatre, like the one which had opened at Finsbury Park in 1930, but what eventually arrived was a Gaumont Palace, operated by Associated Provincial Picture Houses, a subsidiary of the Gaumont-British Corporation.

Entrance to the Gaumont Palace seen shortly after opening in 1934.
(Cinema Theatre Association Archive)

The architect was William Edward Trent, the principal Gaumont architect, working with Ernest Tulley. The entrance façade is relatively narrow, but an imposing set of steps leads to a long, spacious foyer, styled and decorated in the fashionable art-deco style. Further steps lead up to the large circle foyer, and passages lead down to the ground-floor stalls area. Inside, the auditorium is vast, originally seating 2556 patrons – 1,742 in the stalls and 814 in the circle.

The most prominent feature is the pro-

The interior of the Gaumont Palace, showing the organ in the raised position, and the unusual proscenium arch. *(Allen Eyles Collection)*

scenium arch, some 40 ft high and 54ft wide, with a semi-circular shape, formed of two separate circles, the space between being illuminated by concealed lighting. There were round-headed, forward-leaning arches, or lunettes, above the side exits either side of the proscenium. This semi-circular shape of the proscenium was unusual, and may have derived from a well-known German cinema, the Titania-Palast in Berlin which had opened in 1926.

In order to present variety acts as well as films, there was a sizeable stage, with a tall fly-tower (still very noticeable from the High Road) and eight dressing rooms. A highly-decorated safety curtain, depicting the signs of the Zodiac, was designed by Frank Barnes, and is still in situ, hidden from view in the fly-tower.

In the orchestra pit was a British-built Compton theatre

Programme cover for Wood Green Gaumont Palace, November 1934.
(Kevin Phelan Collection).

organ, with the playing console on a rise and fall lift so it could be dropped out of view when films were shown. The organ's specification was of 3 manuals (keyboards) and 12 ranks (sets) of pipes, which were located in 2 rooms beneath the front of the stage. The console had a unique electro-pneumatic action to help the organist select the ranks of pipes he wanted to play. The organ was of a high enough standard to be broadcast on the wireless by the BBC on several occasions, for example in July 1946 it featured in the programme Keyboard Cavalcade with Jack Dowle at the console.

A restaurant with 170 seats was located above the entrance foyer at second-floor level, with access directly from the street via a door beside the main entrance, or from the circle foyer. 3-course suppers were advertised for 1/6d (7 $^{1}/_{2}$p)

The opening night was a spectacular affair, with the Mayor of Wood Green performing the ceremony and a personal appearance by film star Ralph Lynn. The opening films were *The Constant Nymph* starring Victoria Hopper and Brian Aherne, and *Love, Honour and Oh! Baby* with Zasu Pitts and Slim Summerville. On the stage were Bobby Howell and his Band, "in a spectacular naval scene" with the singer Val Rosing. Frederic Bayco was at the Compton organ.

Soon after the Second World War, the word "Palace" was gradually dropped from the cinema's name, becoming plain Gaumont, in line with other cinemas in the circuit.

In 1947, David Goodman was appointed as the manager

at the Gaumont, a position he stayed in for 20 years. In the heyday of the super-cinemas, the cinema manager was an important figure in the local community. They were encouraged to continually promote their cinema and keep it in the public eye each week by arranging publicity stunts, publicising personal appearances by film stars and other activities. David Goodman rose to this challenge with notable success, winning several showmanship awards from his employers, including Rank Showman of the Year in 1954. He continually tried to keep the Gaumont in the local press by arranging countless publicity opportunities. He arranged for numerous exhibitions, such as art and photographic displays, to be held in the large circle foyer area, as Wood Green lacked a suitable venue for many of these. So successful were these that David was selected to serve on the Wood Green Society of Arts, and later he was co-opted onto the Arts and Civic Committee of Wood Green Council, although not an elected councillor. He was also a prominent Rotarian.

This author can remember, as a child, visiting a road safety exhibition at the cinema, staffed by two stern-looking uniformed police officers. He remembers being very frightened when he failed to get all the correct answers in a road-safety quiz! He also remembers David's firm and steady manner at the cinema – you wouldn't dream of misbehaving when he was there, especially during the very popular Saturday morning children's shows.

Comedy actors Stanley Baxter and Leslie Phillips make a personal appearance at the Gaumont to publicise the film "Father Came Too" in 1964. Manager David Goodman can be seen between the two at the rear. *(Authors collection)*

In September 1962, the cinema's name changed to Odeon – the Gaumont and Odeon chains had been jointly controlled by Rank for some years and this change reflected the importance of the Odeon name. By now the restaurant had closed and been converted to a school of dancing with access from the cinema blocked.

In 1967, the cinema underwent a major modernisation involving removing some of the light fittings in the auditorium, covering over some signs and fixtures, and installing a wider screen, which involved cutting into the distinctive proscenium shape. Happily, the changes were not as drastic as in some other cinemas, and enough of the original decoration remained to remind of past glories. The organ was removed at this time too, and was re-installed in Twickenham College of Technology, but it later moved to Thorngate Hall in Gosport, Hampshire, where it is still used for concerts and dances on a few occasions each year. David Goodman also left Wood Green in 1967 and went for a quieter life at the Odeon, Norwich until retirement in 1972. He continued to live in Norfolk until his death in 2001 at the age of 94.

The Odeon continued to be popular, but suffered from the general decline in cinema-going, and in 1973 underwent the "tripling" process to provide a greater choice of films. Two mini-cinemas were created underneath the circle overhang by dropping a new wall from the circle front. These two cinemas, screens 2 and 3, each seated 150, with 814 seats remaining in the original circle, now known as screen 1, which continued to use the existing screen. A new projection box was built at the rear of the former stalls. Some seats were left in the original front stalls area, accessed by a new passage to one side, but in practice were seldom used.

The new 3-screen cinema re-opened on December 30th 1973, and another new feature was a licenced bar in the circle foyer – never very busy in the author's experience – and there was also the novelty of a mobile trolley service for the two mini-cinemas so you could enjoy a drink whilst you watched the film- in a plastic container of course!

But the decline in attendances continued, and the cinema closed on January 7th 1984 – just 2 months before its 50th anniversary. Although still a busy cinema, receipts were not considered high enough to pay for the much needed redecoration that some areas of the building needed. Rank judged the building would be more profitable as a bingo club. The closing films were *Mickey's Christmas Carol* and a revival of Disney's *The Jungle Book* in screen 1, with *Krull* showing in both screens 2 and 3.

Work started immediately on conversion to a Top Rank bingo club, which involved removing the mini-cinemas and inserting a raised false floor in the stalls to create a level area for bingo tables. The front of the balcony was also rebuilt in a terrace pattern to take bingo tables, and a large scoreboard occupied the screen space where films had once appeared. The remainder of the building had a repaint, lighting was restored in many areas and old signs, such as "Circle" and "Stalls" were uncovered. To their great credit, Rank did a splendid job of restoration – the building was unlisted at this time, and they could have simply covered or removed all the decorations and fittings, but they did not.

The bingo club launched on 4th September 1984 and was immediately successful (although Rank closed the nearby clubs at Edmonton and Finsbury Park to boost attendances, and for a few weeks brought their former patrons to Wood Green on a free coach service). In 1990 the building was listed at Grade II.

In 1993 the building was redecorated throughout in a bright new colour scheme, and there were some internal alterations to layout. As these now required Listed Building Consent, one result was the reappearance of the Gaumont Palace name on the front of the building in its original location (and almost the original style of lettering). It is rumoured that this was the result of a "trade-off" with the planning authorities – the internal alterations were approved as long as the old name went back.

Unfortunately, only 3 years later in July 1996, bingo ceased and moved to a former warehouse-style D.I.Y store in Lordship Lane, reopening there as the Mecca Club the same month. The main reason for the move was that the new location offered step-free access and a less expensive building to maintain. Bingo attendances had declined since the launch of the National Lottery in 1994 and new ways had to be found to attract patrons.

The old cinema was boarded up, although the former restaurant area continued to operate, as the Avenida banqueting suite, and then KO nightclub. This at least did mean the frontage

The Gaumont
Palace today

(Poter Staveley)

The restored interior
photographed in
2009.

(Peter Staveley)

was maintained and painted, although for a period in 2006 it was unattractively repainted in all-over black! Several proposals for the closed building came and went, including a nightclub, a rock music venue and a place of worship, even a cinema again, but all came to nothing and it was to remain closed for 7 years. During this time, in 2000, the listing of the building was raised to II*.

Then on 29th May 2004, a local religious group, Edmonton Temple, re-opened the old Gaumont as the Dominion Centre (UPG Ministries) and they use the building as a bookshop, café, and meeting hall and function rooms. They redecorated and restored the former foyer areas, and at first they only utilised the space under the circle as their meeting hall. But in November 2009 they completed a major restoration of the main auditorium, restoring the semi-circular proscenium opening and reinstating the sloping floor to the stalls, and removing the bingo tables in the circle. The splendour of the vast auditorium can be enjoyed once again.

The nightclub operation continues in the former café area.

Barry Took (1928-2002), the comedian and writer, worked at the Gaumont in 1944 and recalls in his autobiography *Point of View*:

"I was bored with working nine to five packing music and got a job as a cinema projectionist in the Gaumont Palace Cinema in Wood Green. I enjoyed life there and as we didn't start until midday and had a day and a half day (from 5pm) off, the work wasn't onerous. I was able to concentrate on trumpet practice in the mornings and fell easily into the pattern of working when other more sober citizens weren't. Watching films five-and-a-half days a week, I learned something of the techniques of film-making but also became deeply aware of how awful many of the films were. On Sundays we had a different programme altogether, generally some obscure melodrama or detective story, old films often close to disintegration on which a close eye had to be kept to prevent the film leaping off the projector and cascading over the projection-room floor. When that did happen, as it did not infrequently, the booth was a scene of wild disorder while the audience booed and stamped until we got the thing going again. Our greatest mistake was to show two reels of a Disney cartoon, 'The Three Caballeros'

upside down and backwards. It was the chief projectionist's day off and his assistant was responsible for the error, but we all got a sound ticking-off from the manager and later on a stiff reprimand from head office."

David Goodman (1907-2001), was manager at the Gaumont from 1947-67, and writing in *Picture House* magazine in 2000 he recalled:
"After the war I went back to the Regent Stamford Hill, but I had nowhere to live and I knew there was a flat at the Gaumont Wood Green – they used to build these into the premises. There was a war-time manager sitting there, so they pushed him out and they gave it to me where I remained for nearly 20 years. A very happy time I had there in Wood Green. I had a big foyer and put on all manner of exhibitions – hobbies, local artists – even a dog show! We had many appearances of film stars – I remember Bill Owen and a very young Dilys Laye – who both lived locally- came to promote 'Trottie True' in 1949, then we had Joan Collins (when she was 17), Dirk Bogarde, Margaret Lockwood, Jack Warner, Hattie Jacques.. and Eamon Andrews once sat outside in an old car to promote 'Genevieve'."

Amanda Smith, who now lives in St. Albans, remembers going to Saturday morning children's shows at the Gaumont in the 1960s:
"One week it was announced that there would be a fancy-dress competition the following Saturday and we were all asked to come dressed as pirates. I was very keen on dressing-up, and persuaded my reluctant younger brother to also participate. Luckily we lived close to the cinema, so did not have many streets to walk through in our home-assembled costumes, which consisted mainly of scarves, earrings and brightly coloured blouses. Out of the large audience of a couple of hundred or so, only me, my brother and one other boy had bothered to dress up. We all won prizes which were presented to us in the manager's, office, so luckily we did not have the embarrassment of going up on stage to receive them in front of the boisterous audience."

CINEWORLD

Unit 19 Shopping City, High Road, Wood Green, N22 6YA

Opened 11th August 2000.

This cinema is unique in our area in having no exterior street entrance – it is entered on the first floor of the extensive indoor shopping centre, known as Shopping City, but also known as The Mall, and is only approached by lifts or escalators. There are prominent illuminated signs outside on the tallest buildings to announce its presence to the unaware.

The 3-storey building housing the 12 auditoria was erected in early 2000 on part of a service yard adjoining Noel Park Road. A disused elevated ramp which had been built to carry traffic from a proposed relief road into the multi-storey car park was demolished to provide extra space. The upper floor of W.H. Smith's shop was sacrificed to provide space for the entrance and

The entrance to the Cineworld multiplex on the upper level of Wood Green Shopping City.
(Peter Staveley)

foyer areas – they gained extra room on the ground floor to compensate. The construction of this cinema came as somewhat of a surprise, because, as recounted later in this book, a purpose-built multi-screen cinema had already been completed earlier that year a short distance away in the High Road, and was lying empty awaiting an operator.

The operator of the new cinema was Cineworld Cinemas Ltd, which had opened their first multiplex cinema in 1996 at Stevenage. Through a series of acquisitions, including the UCG chain, the company is currently the second largest cinema chain in Britain after Odeon, with 75 cinemas in the UK.

At Wood Green, patrons enter the large foyer, and pass the usual ticket desks, popcorn stands and games area. The largest cinemas – screens 1, 2 and 3 – are located on this level. Screen 3 is designated a "deluxe" screen with a supplement on the ticket price, and has its own dedicated foyer with a bar, although it is rarely in operation, and a more luxurious seating layout, with extra space and reclining backs. It is also equipped to show 3-D films.

To reach the remaining 9 smaller cinemas, patrons descend by escalator to the ground floor where the auditoria are arranged off two corridors. All of the cinemas are designed on "stadium" seating lines- the first few rows of seats nearest the screen are on a flat floor, the remainder are then arranged on a stepped area to provide better sightlines. The total seating capacity of the 12 cinemas is 2,250. The large projection room, which serves all the screens, is located on the third floor.

The cinema has proved very successful, being well-placed to attract tired shoppers for their evening relaxation, and also those from further afield who can use the extensive car-parking and reach the cinema by lift without going outdoors. The films on offer always include several foreign-language titles, especially the so-called "Bollywood" Hindi-language products, and Turkish films. There are also popular shows for children on Saturday mornings and special screenings for senior citizens.

Cineworld often hosts special events, such as the Wood Green International Short Film Festival, which has taken place each March since 2003.

SHOWCASE CINEMAS / VUE CINEMAS

Hollywood Green, 180 High Road, Wood Green, N22 6EJ

Opened 11th September 2001

This impressive glass-fronted building opposite Wood Green tube station was the first purpose-built multi-screen cinema to be built in the borough- though not the first to open as it turned out.

The prominent site, long known as Spouters Corner, had become somewhat run-down by the 1970s, a mixed collection of buildings including public toilets, an undertakers premises, a flower and plant merchants, and a row of Victorian houses. In the Haringey Central Area Plan, first published in 1969 and revised in 1976, all would be swept away and replaced by an enlarged road junction and an office development to be called Forum House. But apart from the demolition of the Victorian houses, nothing much happened to the site for many years.

Eventually, in 1996 plans were announced for a "leisure centre" on the site, to include a multiplex cinema, bars and restaurants. Planning permission was given in April 1997 once initial worries by the Council about the lack of on-site car-parking were overcome. All the remaining buildings on the site were levelled soon afterwards, including the former cinema building in Lordship Lane, dating from 1909. The public were asked to suggest a name for the new centre, and "Hollywood Green" was decided upon – a neat combination of the film aspect of the centre and its location. The operator of the 6-screen cinema was to be Hoyts Cinemas Ltd – a large Australian-based cinema chain which was planning to establish a circuit in the UK. This would be their second UK property, having opened a 13-screen cinema at the Bluewater Shopping Centre near Dartford, Kent in March 1999.

The new building was completed by May 2000, and the occupants of the bars and restaurants on the ground floor moved in. But the cinema remained closed, and it became known that

The Hollywood Green building at Wood Green which houses the Showcase / Vue cinemas, photographed in 2008. *(Kake L. Pugh)*

Hoyts had changed their mind about entering the UK market, and were looking to dispose of their Bluewater site and the unopened Wood Green site as well. They had, by then, already signed a lease with the owners of Hollywood Green, and were looking to transfer this lease to another cinema operator.

There was a long delay whilst the transfer was arranged – apparently, Hoyts would only consider an operator who wanted both Bluewater and Wood Green. In the meantime, another multi-screen cinema, operated by a different company – Cineworld – was constructed in Wood Green, a short distance away in Shopping City, which opened in August 2000. Eventually, Hoyts entered into a management agreement with Showcase Cinemas to open and operate the Wood Green cinema, although they retained the lease.

Showcase Cinemas was the trading name of National Amusements, a large family-owned American company which ran a successful chain of cinema in the USA, and had already established a small circuit in the UK. The Wood Green cinema finally opened on 11th September 2001 – unfortunately the day of the terrorist attacks on New York and Washington, which must have put some gloom over the proceedings.

Entering the cinema from the corner of Lordship Lane and the High Road, patrons ascend escalators to the large first-floor foyer area which commands a good view over the street below. Beyond the usual ticket counter and confectionery stands, the 6 separate auditoriums are arranged, all on the same level. They vary in size from 440 seats in the largest to 125 in the smallest, with a total capacity on opening day of 1,779. There is one large projection-box, at an upper level, serving all 6 screens.

The 12-screen Cineworld complex nearby had by now been established for over a year, and with it's convenient on-site car parking it might be thought that the new, smaller Showcase would struggle to find business. But this proved not to be the case, and the cinema has traded successfully since opening- maybe because of its more prominent position opposite the station compared to the rather hidden entrance to Cineworld. The cinema-going population have benefited from the two multiplexes being so close as the competition has kept ticket prices to a low level compared to some other areas of London.

In November 2007, Cineworld announced that they were interesting in acquiring the cinema at Hollywood Green to operate in addition to their existing cinema nearby. The matter was referred to the Office of Fair Trading because it was felt that it would eliminate the competition between the two concerns and this could lead to higher ticket prices. The OFT in turn referred the case to the Competition Commission, but the matter went no further and Showcase remained in control.

Then in 2008, Showcase decided to dispose of their cinemas in the UK and tried to find a buyer for the chain. This proved difficult, but in November 2009, the Wood Green operation was acquired by Vue Cinemas, the third-largest cinema operator in the UK, with 68 cinemas nationwide. Their nearest existing cinema to Haringey is at Finchley.

The last night of Showcase operation was November 30th 2009 and the cinema re-opened under the Vue name on December 17th 2009. Vue have made some improvements, including adding the digital technology to enable 3-D films to be shown, and installing some luxury "VIP" seats, with more space and a leather finish, into all 6 auditoria. This has reduced the seating capacity slightly to a total of 1,720. Another innovation is that selected screenings are for over-18s only, regardless of the censor's certificate for the film. One of the films on re-opening night was *Avatar*, shown in 3-D, widely reported to be one of the most expensive films ever produced, costing some 237 million dollars, but which went on to become the highest-grossing film of all time.

It is unlikely that many of today's patrons in screen 6 realise that they are watching films in almost the same location as people did back in 1910 when the Lordship Lane Cinematograph Theatre occupied part of the site.

Some other places in the area where films were shown:

ALEXANDRA PALACE THEATRE

Alexandra Palace Way, Wood Green, N22 7AY

The theatre was built in 1875 as part of the second Alexandra Palace building, the architect being John Johnson. In the 1890s it was often the home of various forms of travelling "animated entertainments", such as Poole's Myriorama, a form of moving tableau or panorama. In 1901, the first moving pictures were shown, amongst the variety acts, and eventually, the theatre was devoted almost full-time to film entertainment. In 1907, the theatre had to close for nearly 2 years as it was considered unsafe, but by the end of 1908 it had resumed its life as an Electric Theatre, with the projector now housed in a separate room and other safety improvements made.

The *Weekly Herald* of December 12th 1909 states that the "animated pictures at Alexandra Palace used electricity for the first time" – presumably the projectors had utilised a gas-powered generator before this. A typical advertisement from 1913 states "In the Electric Theatre, daily from 3.30 to 10, Sunday 6 to 10, continuous show of the largest and best Animated Pictures-change of programme every Monday, Thursday and Sunday. Popular prices- Adults 6d (2^1/2p) and 3d (1^1/2p) and children 3d and 2d". Films ceased when the War broke out in 1914, and never resumed full-time.

The theatre was eventually acquired by the BBC for use as a scenery store, but nowadays is empty and disused, in need of a full restoration. In June 2003, the Cinema Theatre Association presented a silent film show in the theatre, with piano accompaniment, and a couple of electronic organ concerts have also taken place.

Film entertainment still takes place at the Palace, but in a different area, because each year in the Great Hall silent films are shown, accompanied on the mighty Willis organ by Donald Mackenzie, house organist from the Odeon, Leicester Square. There have been several re-development plans for the Palace since the second big fire of 1980, and these have nearly all included a multiplex cinema, but none of the plans has ever been realised.

ASSEMBLY ROOMS (Wood Green)

242 High Road, Wood Green, N22 8JX
(Entrance in White Hart Lane)

This hall, at the rear of the Kings Arms pub, was used for a wide variety of meetings, concerts, and functions. It was where the first moving-picture show in North London was presented on March 6th 1899.

The local press for 17th February 1899 carried the announcement of "Will Day's Grand Bohemian Concert "and

The Kings Arms Hotel, Wood Green, with the Assembly Rooms at the rear, photographed around 1903.   *(Bruce Castle Museum (Haringey Culture, Libraries and Learning))*

amongst a long list of singers, musicians and comic turns is the item: "Cinematograph – introducing all the latest living pictures, during the performance of which selections will be played on the gramaphone *(sic)* thus combining two of Edison's great inventions".

A report of the concert in *The Sentinel* of March 10th says that the films were very popular, "especially R.W. Paul's film of The Derby". This film had been made in June 1896 by Robert Paul, a pioneer film-maker who lived in Muswell Hill.

Will Day (1873-1936) was one of the first people to operate a film projector in the UK- he was also adept at doing comic turns and monologues as part of his concerts.

The projector used at Wood Green was manufactured by the Wrench Company. Will Day also gave early film shows locally at the Hornsey Wood Tavern, near Finsbury Park, and at Olympia Gardens, Harringay. This was a small pleasure gardens next to the Queens Head pub in Green Lanes – adjacent to the site where one of the area's first cinemas, the Premier Electric – would later be built in 1910. He later went on to operate his own cinema in Wood Green (see entry for Stuart Hall) and then went on to manage a cinema supply company. He was an early collector of pioneering film equipment, and his collection was of such importance that it was donated to the Science Museum after his death, but in 1959 it was transferred to the Cinematheque Francaise in Paris because of its connection to the early French film-makers, the Lumieres.

The Assembly Rooms became a regular cinema in 1909- an advertisement from May promises "Animated Pictures and Parker's Lyric Orchestra, twice nightly at 7 and 9. Special Sunday shows – pictures and music at 8, in aid of cottage hospital". But other functions continued in the hall as well between film times, and gradually the cinema operation became more spasmodic, until by 1910 an advertisement was offering "continuous picture shows every Saturday from 3.30 to 10 but with added varieties occasionally". The last mention seems to have been in the 1916 *Kinematograph Year Book*.

The Assembly Rooms have since gone through many uses, ranging from discotheque to nightclub, but are currently known as the Grand Palace Banqueting Suite. This name has also been applied to the former Kings Arms pub in front.

STUART HALL

22 Stuart Crescent, Wood Green, N22 5NN

This large Victorian House, once numbered 2, Lawn Villas, had been occupied by Wood Green Liberal Club, who had constructed a meeting hall in the back garden. The Liberals moved out in 1908, and in *The Sentinel* for October 30th 1908 appeared the announcement: "Now Open: Stuart Hall, High Road Wood Green, Top of Jolly Butchers Hill. Grand Bioscope Entertainment, in the Large Hall seating 200. Monday, Friday and Saturday evenings at 6, two matinees Saturday 2.30 and 4. Hall can also be hired for functions".

The man behind this venture was Will Day, who had given the film show at the Assembly Rooms in 1899, mentioned earlier.

By the end of 1908, press advertising was also promising "Free admission to the Winter Garden, with Automated Amusements, Refreshment Bar and Lounge. Grand Bioscope Entertainment in large hall at rear. One hour's duration".

But there was no advertising after January 1909, and this early cinema seems to have been a failure financially. The building became Hollingsworth's Estate Office for many years, but is now used as a house and offices. The shape of the hall in the back garden can still be seen from Pellatt Grove, having been converted into living accommodation with its own entrance in Pellatt Grove.

WOOD GREEN EMPIRE

6-7 Cheapside, High Road, Wood Green, N22 6HH

This large variety theatre, seating some 3000, and designed by eminent architect Frank Matcham, opened on September 9th 1912. From the start it was equipped with a projection room and "The Bioscope" was part of the entertainment amongst the list of variety "turns". It was particularly valuable during the First World War when "The War in Pictures" was a regular feature. By 1913, the Empire was opening on Sundays just to show films, the first venue in Wood Green to do so on that day, attracting much opposition in the local press.

The Empire was ahead of all the other local cinemas in installing equipment for sound films – and the first talkie was *The Singing Fool* starring Al Jolson, on August 19th 1929. The local paper, *The Sentinel*, reported on this installation at much length, mentioning "the 3 speakers, each 5ft square and 350 lbs each, on steel towers on ballbearings. There is a new screen and 19 valves at £7.00 each, and it takes 5 men to work the talkie apparatus. Installation has cost the management not a few hundreds but some thousands of pounds". This is no doubt why the Empire was the first to install sound, being owned by Oswald Stoll, a man of some means. A new projection box was also installed and the seating layout altered to remove the division between balcony and gallery.

Speakers and screen had to be designed so that they

A1932 publicity stunt on the pavement outside the Wood Green Empire to publicize the film "With Cobham to Kivu". The film was about an aerial voyage to Africa.

could be moved out of the way for stage acts to perform- hence the ballbearings on the speaker tower – because films did not take over entirely. A week of films seemed to alternate with a week of variety, and in later years, there were sometimes films in the afternoon and variety in the evening. "Visual Education films for Young People" were often shown on Saturday mornings at 11.00 a.m.

But in 1937, the Empire reverted to full-time live variety- by that time two new, purpose-built cinemas, the Gaumont Palace and the Ritz had opened nearby to attract cinema patrons away. The Empire finally closed in January 1955, and was then used as television recording studios for many years. The auditorium was demolished in 1970 for a supermarket and multi-storey car park with flats above, but traces of the High Road frontage can still be seen above the Halifax premises.

REFERENCES

Information has been obtained from the following sources:

BOOKS

DRAPER, Chris: "Islington's Cinemas & Film Studios", Borough of Islington, 1988

ESSEX-LOPESTRI, Michael (editor): "Phoenix East Finchley", 2002.

EYLES, Allen: "ABC-The First name in Entertainment", CTA,.1993
"Gaumont British Cinemas", CTA, 1996.
"Odeon Cinemas, Volumes 1 and 2",
CTA, 2002 and 2005

GAY, Ken: "Muswell Hill-A History and Guide", History Press, 2002

GRAY, Richard: "Cinemas in Britain", Lund Humphries, 1996

McANDREW, Marlene: "Lost Theatres of Haringey", HHS, 2007

PINCHING, Albert: "Wood Green Past", Historical Publications, 2000

PYKE, Chris: "My Search for Montagu Pyke", Snoek Publishing, 2009

WEBB, Malcolm: "Amber Valley Gazeteer of Greater London Suburban Cinemas", Amber Valley, 1986.

Kinematograph Year Books, various years.

Extract from "Point of View" by Barry Took reproduced with permission of Duckworth & Co Publishers.

Extract from "Yealm" by Sheila Lahr reproduced with permission from *militantesthetics.com*

PERIODICALS

PICTURE HOUSE – the magazine of the Cinema Theatre Association, particularly
Issue 24 "The Oldest Cinema" by Martin Tapsell.
Issue 25 "Two Gaumont Managers",
Issue 31 "Essoldo Cinemas" by Frank Manders and Charles Morris
Issue 32 "Edward A.. Stone" by Ken George.

HORNSEY HISTORICAL SOCIETY Bulletin Issue 40.
"The (mostly lost) Cinemas of Haringey" by Ken Gay

CINEMA THEATRE ASSOCIATION Bulletins. Various issues.

CINEMA ORGAN SOCIETY Newsletter and Journal. Various issues.

IDEAL KINEMA, THE BIOSCOPE and KINEMATOGRAPH WEEKLY. Various issues

TOTTENHAM & WOOD GREEN WEEKLY HERALD, HORNSEY JOURNAL, MUSWELL HILL RECORD, THE SENTINEL. Various issues.

MEMORY LANE: Issue 162

ARCHIVES
Borough of Haringey Local Studies Archive, Bruce Castle Museum, Tottenham, N17, and local history collection at Hornsey Library.

London Metropolitan Archives, EC1, particularly the files of the former Middlesex County Council.

The Cinema Museum, London SE11.

Cinema Theatre Association, London, E10.

BFI Library, London, WC1.

British Library Newspaper Library, London, NW9.

Hornsey Historical Society, London, N8.

WEBSITES
(Consulted between June 2008 and January 2010)

CINEMA TREASURES: cinematreasures.org (particularly the contributions of Ken Roe)

THE LONDON PROJECT: http://londonfilm.bbk.ac.uk/ (the work of Ian Christie, Simon Brown and Luke McKernan)

INTERNET MOVIE DATABASE: www.imdb.com
http://www.dermon.com/Beatles/details/tours
http://www.thewholive.de/konzerte/zeige_konzert.php

WHO'S WHO IN VICTORIAN CINEMA (victorian-cinema.net)

HARRINGAYONLINE – particularly the writings of Hugh Flouch

THANKS ALSO for help, advice, photos and checking of facts: Allen Eyles, Ken Gay, Richard Gray, Tim Hatcher, Brian Hornsey, Richard Norman, Gerald Smith, Peter Staveley, David Warner, Kevin Wheelan.

THE CINEMA THEATRE ASSOCIATION (founded 1967) is for those with a serious interest in cinema architecture. It publishes a bi-monthly newsletter, an annual magazine, organises visits to interesting cinemas, and maintains an extensive archive. It also campaigns for the preservation of our finest cinemas. Details at *www.cinema-theatre. org.uk*, or contact the membership secretary, Neville Taylor, at Flat 1, 128, Gloucester Terrace, London, W2 6HP.

Index of Cinemas